CARMELITE MONASTERY
68 FRANKLIN AVENUE
SARANAC LAKE, NEW YORK

THE
MIRACLE
OF THE
MOUNTAIN

THE STORY

OF BROTHER ANDRÉ

AND THE SHRINE

ON MOUNT ROYAL

by

ALDEN HATCH

ILLUSTRATED

HAWTHORN BOOKS, INC., *Publishers*

NEW YORK

THE

MIRACLE

OF THE

MOUNTAIN

CARMELITE MONASTERY
68 FRANKLIN AVENUE
SARANAC LAKE, NEW YORK

© 1959 BY HAWTHORN BOOKS, INC., 70 FIFTH AVENUE, NEW YORK 11.
COPYRIGHT UNDER INTERNATIONAL AND PAN-AMERICAN COPYRIGHT CON-
VENTIONS. ALL RIGHTS RESERVED, INCLUDING THE RIGHT TO REPRODUCE
THIS BOOK, OR PORTIONS THEREOF, IN ANY FORM, EXCEPT FOR THE INCLU-
SION OF BRIEF QUOTATIONS IN A REVIEW. THIS BOOK WAS MANUFACTURED
IN THE UNITED STATES OF AMERICA AND PUBLISHED SIMULTANEOUSLY
IN CANADA BY MCCLELLAND & STEWARD, LTD., 25 HOLLINGER ROAD,
TORONTO 16. LIBRARY OF CONGRESS CATALOGUE CARD NUMBER 59–6878.
FOURTH PRINTING, MAY, 1962

The Library of Congress has catalogued this book as follows:

Hatch, Alden, 1898—
    The miracle of the mountain; the story of Brother André and
the shrine on Mount Royal. ₁1st ed.₁ New York, Hawthorn
Books ₁1959₁

    224 p. illus. 24 cm.

    1. André, Brother, 1845–1937.   1. Title.

BX4705.A58H3   922.271   59–6878 ‡

    Library of Congress

To
Father Roland Gauthier, C.S.C., Father Henry Bernard, C.S.C.
and all the priests and brothers of Holy Cross, as well
as the many laymen, who helped me because they loved
Brother André so much, this book is gratefully dedicated.

Contents

THE
MIRACLE
OF THE
MOUNTAIN

PROLOGUE

A Servant Passes

THERE could hardly have been a man more humble than the little lay brother of the Congregation of Holy Cross who lay dying in the Hospital of Notre-Dame de l'Espérance at Saint Laurent in the ragged northern outskirts of Montreal on the night of January 5, 1937. His tiny body, exhausted by illness and great age, seemed childlike in the narrow, white-painted iron bedstead. His material possessions were a patched soutane for every day and a good one for Sundays, a missal, a Bible, *The Imitation of Christ* by Thomas à Kempis, three holy statues, and the Saint Joseph's medal that hung around his neck outside the white hospital nightgown.

In all his long life of ninety-one years, Brother André had never owned very much more than this. He was a child of poverty who had not even learned to read or write until he had joined the Order in his twenties. Naturally, with so little schooling and his impaired health he could not have easily acceded to the priesthood. Indeed, he was thankful and felt honored to be allowed to perform the most menial work of his community, to serve God and Saint Joseph in the lowliest capacity.

The little hospital to which he had been taken from his cell

[11]

at Saint Joseph's Oratory six days before was quite in keeping with his condition. It was a small brick building with rickety wooden porches and some twenty or thirty rooms. The room he occupied was perhaps ten feet long by eight feet wide. It had white wooden walls, a little bedside table, a wooden chair, a corner shelf, and three hooks to hang clothes on. That night it was the focus of attention of all Montreal—Catholic, Protestant and Jew—and, indeed, of a large portion of the North American Continent.

In the city rooms of the great Montreal papers, editors held the presses waiting for news from that room. All the radio stations broadcasted hourly bulletins. The Crypt-Chapel of Saint Joseph's Oratory on Mount Royal was crowded with people praying for the little brother. Outside the hospital thousands of the faithful knelt in the icy night. The hospital was congested with hundreds of Brother André's personal friends who had come to visit him. Ever since he had lapsed into a coma early that morning they had been there. On the orders of Dr. Lionel Lamy and Father Albert Cousineau, Superior of Saint Joseph's Oratory, they had been admitted one by one to Brother André's room—since their presence could not tire him now—to look for a last time, and touch his hand in farewell; and perhaps to gain some of the spiritual grace that seemed to emanate from his unconscious form.

At eleven thirty in the evening a crisis came in his illness. The three doctors in attendance gathered quickly by his bed. Father Cousineau, and all the religious, and Brother André's lay friends fell on their knees. Then Dr. Lamy, his personal physician, spoke. "Brother André will not leave us yet," he said. "He will wait until tomorrow which is a day consecrated to Saint Joseph."

Fifty minutes after midnight on January 6, Brother André died. As Dr. Lamy pronounced him gone, the Superior of the Oratory rose from his knees and loosing the chain from around his own neck, laid on Brother André's breast the priestly crucifix he might not wear in life.

The Movement for Recognition

Thousands of people who believed they had been cured of grave illnesses by the prayers of Brother André and the intercession of Saint Joseph; tens of thousands who had known him and observed his dedicated life; and hundreds of thousands who had seen him or heard of him were firmly convinced that Brother André was a saint. If they had had their way the little brother would have been canonized by acclamation as he lay in death in the primitive hospital at Saint Laurent.

Once long ago their spontaneous veneration would have been sufficient. But as far back as the tenth century the Holy Catholic Church wisely decided to interpose a rigorous investigation of a man's life and actions before the Pope officially and infallibly declared that he was a saint.

In the course of such an investigation a meticulous, virtually microscopic, examination is made of every circumstance, condition and action—of virtually every thought—of the Servant of God, as he is called, from his first faint wail of life to the ultimate sigh with which he yields his soul to his Creator. Indeed, it goes farther than that; it considers the circumstances of his parents before he was born, and pursues its investigation beyond the grave.

Because of the great spontaneous popular veneration of Brother André, and because he believed that the recognition of his holy life and works would inspire the faithful and redound to the greater glory of God and His Church, Joseph Charbonneau, Archbishop of Montreal, ordered three years later that an informal inquiry be made concerning Brother André's life. The Archbishop felt that he had sufficient information to warrant starting proceedings of beatification and canonization. This he did by writing, on November 13, 1940, a circular letter to his clergy and flock, stating the circumstances and setting up a Tribunal according to canon law to make a formal investigation, with a view to finding witnesses and collecting the writings of Brother André.

The Tribunal began to function in 1941. This preliminary phase continued for nine years. In 1950, the evidence was presented to the Congregation of Sacred Rites in Rome. They in turn sifted and studied it for eight years longer before discussing whether or not the Cause was worthy of the attention of the Holy Father.

Meanwhile, the Summation of the Cause, prepared in Rome for the attention of the Sacred Congregation of Rites, is now available for study. So extraordinary is the story it reveals that no writer of fiction would dare invent it; nor would a biographer record it with the expectation of being believed unless it were backed by the sworn testimony of hundreds of eyewitnesses, the medical records of Protestant as well as Catholic hospitals, and the frankly astonished concurrence of leading physicians in Canada and the United States.

Of Saints . . .

Jesus is the one true Saint, the perfect Man. In the *Gloria in Excelsis* are the words, "You alone are the Holy One . . . You alone, Jesus Christ, are the Most High." But those who by His Grace achieve an unusual measure of holiness are called saints. In his Epistles, Saint Paul refers to all his Christian brothers as saints, meaning that they are sanctified by their acceptance of Jesus Christ. But the term soon came to apply to the Apostles and the early martyrs of the Christian faith. At first, however, they were not referred to as "Saint Peter" or "Saint Paul," for example, but simply by their first names as in the fervent appeal scratched on the walls of the catacombs: "Peter and Paul pray for me." Nevertheless, the belief that the Apostles and the martyrs, being especially beloved by Jesus, could intercede on behalf of a petitioner was an early and perfectly logical conception. Such veneration is called a *cultus* or cult.

The formal use of "Saint" became general in the third century, A.D., and the cultus was rapidly extended to certain Christians who had led especially holy lives and had been given signs of divine favor such as visions and the power to perform miracles. The names of these persons were inscribed by the bishops in the records or canons of their dioceses; hence, the term *canonization.*

Inevitably this informal process led to somewhat wholesale canonization, in the course of which some doubtful characters were named among the elect. As a result the Council of Mainz, in A.D. 813, forbade canonization without the consultation of an episcopal synod. From the year 1000 on, the process of canonization gradually became reserved to the Pope, and the rules governing it became more and more stringent. Finally, in 1634, Pope Urban VIII promulgated the rules of procedure which have been generally followed ever since. These rules, somewhat modernized, were embodied in the codification of canon law authorized by Pope Benedict XV in 1917. It was in accordance with them that the Tribunal to consider the Cause of Brother André was set up in the Archepiscopal Palace in Montreal, in 1941.*

This Tribunal was in fact a legal court of inquiry. It consisted of a judge appointed by the Archbishop and two associate judges. There were also a notary or secretary, and a protonotary. According to the law these gentlemen were obliged to keep the record in longhand, typewriters not being permitted. There was also a *coursier* or messenger to handle the documents. The importance and care attached to every scrap of paper relative to the Cause is indicated by the fact that this office was held by no less a person than Monsieur l'Abbé Paul Touchette.

* Subsidiary tribunals were also set up in Ottawa and Saint Hyacinthe, in Canada, and in Providence, Rhode Island, to take the testimony of many witnesses who had known Brother André in those localities.

The two most active figures in the hearings were the Vice Postulator of the Cause, the Reverend Father Alfred Laplante, C.S.C. (Congregation of Holy Cross), whose function was to plead Brother André's Cause; and Canon Adolphe Sylvestre, the Promoter of the Faith, who was assisted by a sub-promoter, Canon Raoul Drouin. The Promoter of the Faith is generally known as "the Devil's Advocate" and his assistant might be called the Vice Devil's Advocate. Their function was to make sure that every requirement of canon law was strictly followed, and that everything which might be derogatory to Brother André was fully aired. They cross-questioned the witnesses rigorously; endeavored to confuse them, and even asked leading questions—not permitted in civil law—in their efforts to elicit damaging statements. In short, they acted like devil-inspired district attorneys. In so doing they were properly fulfilling their function of making certain that the Servant of God was indeed worthy to be named among the saints.

In order even to prove that the Cause was worthy of the Holy Father's attention, the Tribunal of Montreal had to establish certain things concerning Brother André. These were, in order:

1. His heroic Christian virtue (in general).
2. His heroic faith.
3. His heroic hope of heaven.
4. His heroic love of God.
5. His heroic love of his neighbor.
6. His heroic prudence.
7. His heroic justice.
8. His heroic temperance.
9. His heroic poverty.
10. His heroic chastity.
11. His heroic obedience.
12. His heroic humility.
13. The supernatural gifts and miracles attributed to him in life.

[16]

14. The facts concerning his burial, the concourse of people who spontaneously venerated him in his sepulcher.

15. His fame of sanctity in life and after death.

16. Grace and miracles.

In addition, it had to be proved beyond doubt that no *official* cultus or veneration of Brother André had been permitted. This canon is most strictly enforced because it is vitally important in reserving the function of beatification and canonization to the Pope.

If the Holy Father eventually decides that the Servant of God is worthy, he declares him *Beatus* (Blessed) and directs that he may be venerated in certain specified localities. This title is provisional and may be revoked. To go on to canonization a similar but shorter process must be carried out. The most important part of this canonization process is to prove beyond doubt by eyewitnesses and medical certificates that at least two more miracles have been wrought through the intercession of the Beatus *after* he was beatified. If these are proved the Pope in a special, solemn rite in Saint Peter's Basilica irrevocably and infallibly declares: "To the honor of the holy and undivided Trinity . . . We decree and define that the blessed —— is a saint, and We enter his name in the roll of saints, ordering that his memory be religiously venerated every year by the Church throughout the world."

The Cause

Even before the other members of the Tribunal were appointed the Vice Postulator was busy preparing his case. Indeed he had been hard at work for over three years. It was up to him to prove the facts of Brother André's life. First he must make certain in his own mind that all sixteen of the qualifications for canonization could be *juridically* proved in Brother André's case. Then he must find the means of proving them. This would involve an enormous amount of research. Official documents would have to be obtained or photostated; newspaper

[17]

clippings culled and filed; every possible source of information concerning Brother André's parents and his youth, veiled in the mists of nearly a century, must be examined and produced. All his writings must be collected and studied. This was not difficult in Brother André's case since they consisted of two short letters written to his family.

Then the list of witnesses must be made up. There were a large number of these since the law required that diligent search be made for everyone who knew the Servant of God, his friends and those who may have disliked him—especially the latter. Since thousands of people knew Brother André the Vice Postulator was obliged to interview vast numbers of possible witnesses and winnow out the least important lest the preliminary hearing consume a century or so instead of the nine years it actually took. Finally, in consultation with the Devil's Advocate, he drew up a list of more than two hundred questions to be asked every witness in order to elicit all the facts.

All this cost a great deal of money. The Holy See is not responsible for such expenses. The money was raised, as provided for in canon law, by appealing to those of the faithful who desired to see Brother André canonized. The Vice Postulator had no trouble raising it.

Since beatification and canonization are graces which ultimately come from God, it was also the duty of the Vice Postulator to encourage the people to pray for the success of the Cause. In this also he had no difficulty. The faithful came in thousands to Saint Joseph's Oratory to pray . . . "Most Holy Father and Adorable Trinity, Father, Son and Holy Spirit . . . concede to us the beatification and canonization of our beloved Brother André."

The Future

As to the ultimate result of the nine years of preliminary inquiry, 1941 to 1950, and the eight years of study, from 1950 to 1958, the testimony in Rome—that result is still far in the future. The Pope alone can say whether the cures attributed to Brother André were true miracles or not. He alone can name him worthy to be called Saint.

One thing is certain. Even by the time the preliminary investigation was completed, the entire story of Brother André's simple and marvelous life was on the record.

The First Witness

THE Tribunal to consider the Cause of the Beatification and Canonization of Brother André met in the Archbishop's Palace in Montreal. It stood next to the Cathedral on Dominion Square, which was a peaceful place of trees and fine office buildings in the flat crowded heart of the city between the Saint Lawrence River and the Mountain, which rose steeply to the north bearing on its craggy shoulders the climbing outskirts of Montreal.

Outwardly the palace was a block-long, grim-faced structure; within, it was half office building, half splendid mansion, where the Archbishop lived and the work of the archdiocese was done by a staff of priests and religious.

The Tribunal was headed by Judge Delegate Father Laurent Pellegrino, a Jesuit priest to whom the Archbishop had delegated authority to conduct the hearing. The associate judges were Canons Laurent Morin and Jacques de Marigny. Canon Sylvestre, the Promoter of the Faith, was also an official with high intellectual standards. This was important, for his duties required that his mind must dominate his emotions.

In order to insure impartiality only one representative of Brother André's order (the Congregation of Holy Cross) served on the Tribunal. He was the Vice Postulator, Father Laplante, a man whose high forehead and thin, finely-drawn features suggested his ascetic nature. He alone of the Tribunal had been closely associated with Brother André at the Oratory; and with his own eyes he had seen many remarkable happenings. He was utterly devoted to the little brother. This, too, was important, for on him depended the success of the Cause.

The language of the Tribunal was the slightly archaic French of the Province of Quebec—few of the witnesses spoke English. Written comments of the members of the court were in Latin. The officials were sworn according to the prescribed oath. The Vice Postulator was required to take a special oath. In addition to swearing to fulfill his duty and keep secret all that transpired in the court, he protested that he undertook the Cause of the Servant of God only for the honor and glory of God, and proposed to use only honest means to promote it. The first witness was then called.

He was Monsieur Joseph Pichette, who had been, perhaps, Brother André's closest friend. Pichette was a tall, thin man in his late fifties. He owned a small shoe store in Montreal and had been one of the friends who often drove Brother André to the hospitals to visit the sick, or to the homes of those who were too ill to come to the Oratory. In the course of these visits he had seen many marvelous things, and, indeed, thirty years before he himself had been completely cured of a heart condition which his doctor had described as fatal. Religion was Joseph Pichette's whole life. He was a sweet and simple man who truly believed that Brother André was a saint.

M. Pichette described to this biographer his experiences before the Tribunal that first morning. "I was terribly frightened," he said. "I would have given all the money I had—any amount—to get out of this. When I arrived they took me to the Archbishop's parlor, a huge room with about a hundred chairs around the walls. I thought the Archbishop would be coming in, and then what would I do?"

That was, in fact, the finest salon M. Pichette had ever seen. It had beautiful crystal chandeliers and the walls were hung with fine brocade. At one end of the room was a throne covered by a purple and gold baldachin. Pichette sat there quaking for several minutes until a young priest came and showed him into the room where the hearings were held. It was also large, but plainly furnished. There was a big table around which sat the canons and priests who composed the court. M. Pichette was introduced to them.

Then, since it was the opening session, Archbishop Joseph Charbonneau, who had succeeded Monseigneur Gauthier in Montreal, came in to greet the members of the Tribunal. He was very courteous and friendly. M. Pichette kissed his ring, and felt much easier.

After chatting for a few moments the Archbishop left. The door of the courtroom was then locked, and the *coursier,* l'Abbé Touchette, stationed himself beside it. M. Pichette was given a paper "several feet long" to read aloud. It described the oath he was to take and the penalty for breaking or evading it in any way; to wit: excommunication reserved to the Holy See. Pichette understood that, "This meant that nobody could give you absolution for that sacrilege but the Pope himself. Not the Archbishop or the Cardinal of Quebec. Only the Pope!"

Then Pichette knelt down. He placed his right hand on the Bible and slowly and solemnly repeated the oath:

"I swear to tell all the truth, nothing but the truth, to the advantage of the Servant of God and also that which would be unfavorable to him. Before God and my conscience I have nothing in view but the truth. I will expose it fully and faithfully, changing nothing, omitting nothing. I swear equally never to tell anyone of the questions which were asked me and of the answers I gave, with the help of God and touching the Holy Gospels."*

* M. Pichette was able to describe the scene because the witnesses were absolved from the oath of secrecy when the proceedings were published by the Sacred Congregation of Rites. He says, "I was terribly tempted to tell my wife the questions so she would be prepared to answer them when she was called. But I did not dare."

Then everyone took chairs around the big table except one man who sat at a small separate table furiously taking notes. Pichette did not understand his function at the time.

After the questions which established Pichette's identity and condition, he was asked: *Has anyone instructed you as to what you should say here?*

"No one has instructed me in any way. I am here to tell the truth," Pichette said stoutly.

He was then asked: *When did you meet the Servant of God?*

He replied, "I knew Brother André well for about thirty years. I saw him a hundred or a hundred and fifty times a year. He often came to my house."

When was he born?

"I have knowledge that Brother André was born on August 9, 1845, in Saint Grégoire, in the District of Iberville."

Note the phrase, "I have knowledge." By using it M. Pichette indicated that this was hearsay. "I was careful to swear to nothing which I had not seen with my own eyes, or which Brother André had not told me himself."

Indeed no one alive could testify to anything but hearsay concerning the birth of a child nearly a century before. You may be sure that when the Promoter General of the Faith, in Rome—the head devil's advocate—examined the testimony he made the point that there were no eyewitnesses to the childhood of Brother André, or indeed to any of his activities until he was fifty years old. The postulator disposed of this objection by pointing out that it was impossible for any witnesses of his childhood to have survived.

However, the circumstances were well known. The child, whose name in the world was Alfred Bessette, was born in his father's home about two miles from the hamlet of Saint Grégoire in the Richelieu Valley about thirty miles southeast of Montreal and the same distance from the American border.

The Bessette house was, in fact, no more than a wooden cabin consisting of a single room twenty feet by seventeen. Alfred was the sixth child of his parents. Three more children came later, making eleven in all who lived in that cramped space.

But if the dwelling was primitive it stood in beauty. It was situated at a crossroads in the flat fertile "prairie" clothed in the brilliant green and gold pattern of agriculture. A short distance off, Mount Saint Grégoire humped abruptly out of the level ground as though forced up by a subterranean explosion. The dark green of pine trees growing on its crest provided a cool contrast to the fields of grain which lapped its rocky sides. Two other small unexpected hills, Mounts Beloeil and Hilaire, appeared in the blue distance.

Was the child baptized in the Church?

"I have knowledge that he was."

This was a pro forma question, since the baptism was a matter of record:

> The tenth of August eighteen hundred and forty-five by us, the undersigned priest, was baptized Alfred, born yesterday of the legitimate marriage of Isaac Bessette, carpenter, and Clautilde [sic] Foisy of this parish. The godfather, Edouard Bessette, and the godmother, Josephine Bessette, as well as the father, have declared that they do not know how to sign their names.

This is how it was set down in the register of marriages, births, etc., of Saint-Grégoire-le-Grand.

The certificate does not tell the whole story. The newborn baby was so frail that the experienced midwife said he would live no more than an hour or two. So she hastily baptized him in the informal ceremony which may be performed by any of the faithful in such an emergency. Happily, she underestimated his endurance by almost ninety-two years.

The following day he seemed much stronger, and his father

carried him to the village. There was no consecrated church in Saint-Grégoire-le-Grand; so poor a place it was despite its imposing name. Instead there was a fieldstone building rather like a New England meetinghouse. Weekdays it was a school, evenings the village elders conferred there, and on Sunday a priest set up a portable altar and said Mass. In a room whose walls were lined with blackboards, among the small desks and wooden benches of the school children, Alfred Bessette was officially received into the Church.

Who were the parents of the Servant of God?

Again M. Pichette "had knowledge" of the pro forma question. And again it was a matter of record.

When their little son was born it is doubtful if even Isaac and Clothilde Bessette knew who they were in the sense of family history. But after Brother André's fame had spread so far, Joseph Drouin, one of Canada's leading genealogists, went to great pains to trace his descent.

According to him the founder of the family in Canada was Jean Bessette who was born at Cahors in the South of France. He came to Canada as a soldier in the Carignan Regiment about 1677. Jean Bessette must have been a first-class fighting man, for his comrades nicknamed him *"Brisetout"* (Break everything). When his regiment was recalled to France in 1687, Jean opted for the New World with its wild free life, its deep forests and rich virgin land, its opportunities and its dangers. On July 3, 1688, he married Anne Le Seilgneur who had come from Rouen in France. Brisetout found danger before opportunity. In 1692 he was killed by the Iroquois Indians. But he had founded a numerous and hardy line. Isaac Bessette was the sixth in descent from Brisetout.

Brother André's mother came from an even older French-Canadian family, founded by Martin Foisy, who came to Canada in 1663. Isaac Bessette and Clothilde Foisy were married at Saint Mathias on September 27, 1831.

As is evidenced by his baptismal certificate and the known facts, Alfred Bessette's parents were very humble people. As the family grew in size, Isaac Bessette found it more and more difficult to provide food for them. There was never enough work for a carpenter in that small isolated village. Isaac would have been glad to work much harder for he appears to have loved his trade. It was, later, a source of satisfaction to his son as well; for to Brother André, who loved Saint Joseph so greatly, the fact that his own father had also been a carpenter gave him a mystical sense of closeness to the foster father of our Lord.

The first day's questioning ended at about this point. M. Pichette was given the written transcript of his testimony to read and verify. Then, very ceremoniously, it was taped and sealed with the great seal of the Archbishop.

M. Pichette was told to return on the morrow. Indeed, he went back twenty times or more, and his condensed testimony fills nearly eighty pages of the Summation of the Cause. His simple faith impressed even the devil's advocate, who although he wrote rapidly and ominously did not cross-examine Pichette. In fact, after a while Canon Sylvestre rose abruptly, tore up his notes and threw them in the wastebasket. It was evident that he felt there was no profit in questioning the testimony of a man who was so transparently honest. Either you must accept it whole or dismiss it entirely.

Canon Sylvestre was not as gentle with some of the other witnesses. He gave the brilliant prelates who testified a very rough time indeed, and he sharply attacked the better-educated laymen. One of these was Arthur Ganz, a cultivated, pugnacious Swiss convert to Catholicism. Ganz, like Pichette, did not know Sylvestre's function. He says that, "This man kept contradicting me. He would say, 'I'm sure it did not happen just that way,' or 'Now think carefully. Was it not more like this?' Finally, I got boiling mad and burst out before all those reverend fathers with 'If you think I'm a liar, why did you call me here?'

"At that they burst out laughing and explained that Canon Sylvestre was the devil's advocate, and was only fulfilling his function."

M. Pichette was a very valuable witness. However, other witnesses knew far more about Brother André's childhood and youth; so they will be heard here, out of order, to preserve the chronological sequence of the narrative. M. Pichette will be recalled to the stand in due time.

CHAPTER   T W O

A Crucifix in a Stable

Perhaps the witness closest to Brother André's youth was his
niece, Mme. Attaris Lafleur, daughter of his younger sister, who
testified before the subsidiary tribunal in Rhode Island where
she lived. Madame Lafleur's mother had told her many stories
of her brother's childhood, and when Brother André came to
stay with them in the United States in later life, he often
reminisced with his sister about their youth. However, Madame
Lafleur's testimony leaves many gaps, which may be filled by
other witnesses to whom Brother André spoke of his boyhood.
In addition, Father Henri-Paul Bergeron, C.S.C., made such a
painstaking study of the early life for his biography of Brother
André that parts of the book were admitted as evidence by the
meticulous Sacred Congregation of Rites. Another interesting
witness was Adélard Fabre, a lay workman at the Oratory, to
whom Brother André confided many details of his childhood.

All this is hearsay evidence. Nevertheless, an accurate picture
of that frail little boy of long ago emerges. Especially one may
believe the things that the witnesses swore they had been told
directly by Brother André. For he was, without question, a man
of truth.

What do you know of the Servant of God's upbringing?

To this question Madame Lafleur could reply that her grand-
parents were devout Catholics who taught their children the
simple faith they held. "The whole Bessette family was very

[31]

pious," she said; and added, "Brother André's parents died when he was very young."

Other witnesses filled in the details.

For the first few years of Alfred's life the Bessettes were a very happy family despite their poverty. The gay recollections of their home, which he exchanged with his sister, and which he confided to his friends, show how happy they were. Despite his weak constitution, Alfred was a merry child. Perhaps because Isaac Bessette was away from home so much at his work, Brother André had only a misty recollection of his father. But his memory of his mother was bright and warm.

"My mother, knowing that I was very frail, seemed to have more love and care for me than for the others," he said. "She kissed me more often than was my turn, and frequently gave me little delicacies in secret. In the evening when we recited family prayers I was next to her, and followed the prayers on her rosary.

"In those days I never saw my mother when she was not smiling—and what a lovely smile! Since her death she often smiles at me. She comes and, without speaking, looks lovingly at me. I rarely pray for her, but very often I pray *to* her."

When Alfred was about four years old his father found that he could no longer earn a living in Saint Grégoire. He moved his family to the larger town of Farnham, and set himself up as a wheelwright as well as a carpenter. There were more opportunities in Farnham and for a short while he prospered. In order to earn still more money, Bessette sometimes went out into the woods as a lumberjack.

Like his ancestor Brisetout, Isaac Bessette found death in the forest. One of the great primeval trees that he brought down with his axe fell the wrong way and crushed out his life. He was buried in the cemetery at Farnham.

For four years more courageous Clothilde Bessette somehow held the family together. How she managed to do it is a mystery for which the witnesses offer no solution. It is probable that the older boys were able to bring in a little money; and it is known that members of her family and even the neighbors helped to provide food. But the main burden fell on Clothilde. That she carried it so long is a minor miracle of fortitude and faith.

Overwork and lack of proper food eventually brought on tuberculosis, the great killer-plague of those times. When Clothilde could no longer support the family, it was broken up. The children were taken into the homes of various relatives, and Clothilde went to live in the adjacent town of Saint Césaire with her sister, Mme. Timothée Nadeau, taking only Alfred with her.

That was a sad two years for him. His beloved mother quietly faded out of life still smiling as he recalled. Her last day he remembered very well. When she knew that she was dying, Clothilde asked to see all her children together once more. The kindly aunts and uncles brought them from the scattered villages where they now lived. As is often the case with consumptives, Clothilde was completely lucid in her last moments, perhaps even more acute than she normally was. With perfect courage and in the manner of an era when dying was a thing to be done with a dignified regard for the *conventions,* she made a formal little speech to her children which was forever engraved on Brother André's brain.

"My dear little ones," she said. "It is now six years since your papa left us to go to heaven. The good God is coming to look for me in my turn. Pray for me. Do not forget the tomb of your father. My body will repose beside his in the cemetery at Farnham. From the height of heaven I will watch over you. . . ."

Brother André firmly believed that she kept her word.

What do you know of the education of the Servant of God?

To this question Madame Lafleur answered, "He was not well instructed."

This was an understatement. It is doubtful if as a child

Brother André learned more than to sign his name with enormous effort. He attended school very sporadically, if at all, while his mother lived, because he was seldom well enough to venture outdoors during the bitter Canadian winter. Soon after her death, Timothée Nadeau called his nephew to him and told him that it was time to stop weeping and go to work. "You are twelve years old," he said. "At your age I was earning my own living. You must learn to be independent for we are not rich."

Timothée Nadeau was a robust man and a hard worker. So were all of his children. He was generous but insensitive. As Brother André once remarked; "My uncle was a very strong man and he expected everyone else to be like him."

However, Nadeau was not unreasonable. Brother André recalled that his uncle looked him over and added, "With your feeble health and your withdrawn ways you can't do everything. I think, Alfred, I'll have you taught to be a shoemaker."

So Alfred obediently left the school he had just begun to attend and went to work for the village cobbler. He was not a success. The sensitive little boy, dreaming of his lost mother, missing her spoiling and affection, had no heart for his work though he tried hard. Never having done anything with his hands, he was incredibly clumsy. He squatted all day on a pile of stiff leather trying to turn out the cowhide boots which were his master's best-selling item. He was forever pricking his fingers with the awl and having to be bandaged up so his blood would not smear the hides. In addition, probably more for psychosomatic reasons than from actual fatigue, the weak digestion which he had had all his life grew worse. He had terrible pains in his stomach and could hardly eat at all. As he remarked later, "You understand, working as a cobbler almost on all fours, hammering away all day, is not good for the digestion." However, he was not resentful of his uncle, merely sorry he was such a disappointment, for he loved the Nadeaus deeply.

Fortunately, this particular sojourn in purgatory did not last very long. It is probable that his affectionate aunt begged her husband to find lighter work for Alfred; or possibly the shoemaker got bored with so inept an apprentice. In any event Alfred went to work in the small local bakery. He did much better there.

Life in the Quebec countryside is almost timeless; things change slowly if at all. The *habitants* speak the French of Louis XIV's time, almost incomprehensible to modern Parisians. The bakery where Alfred Bessette worked is still standing and still in business ninety-nine years later. The master baker shoves the molded loaves into the same brick oven that was used then; and the apprentice boy sat on the same stool where Alfred kneaded dough until the proprietor gave it to the Oratory museum as a hallowed treasure a few years ago.

Alfred enjoyed working there. In winter it was kept warm by the crackling wood fire that heated the oven. Sunshine poured through two high windows that looked down the slope to the feed store next door. It smelled like heaven, and still does, with the delicious aroma of baking bread and the sweet fragrance of cakes and pastries. However, this earthly paradise also lasted but a short time for Alfred.

In 1860, a year after Alfred went to work in the bakery, Timothée Nadeau got an unexpected attack of gold fever. He settled his family, including Alfred, in Farnham and headed hopefully for California. It was now more necessary than ever for Alfred to become self-supporting. He got himself a job with a farmer named Ouimet, in whose house he lived. He appears to have worked for his board and keep.

Was the Servant of God pious in his youth?

To this question Madame Lafleur replied, "Yes, he was very pious. Once he asked Father Sylvestre [the Curé of Farnham], 'What prayers give the most pleasure to the good God?' Father Sylvestre replied, 'Our Father' and 'Hail Mary.' This I know because Brother André told me so himself."

Father Bergeron, replying to the same question, testified that Brother André's sister said to him, "Ah, if you had known my brother in his youth! On Sunday he passed the greater part of the afternoon praying in the church."

Religion had played an important part of Alfred Bessette's life since the cradle. However, his great devotion to God may well have begun with the tragic death of his father and deepened during his mother's long illness. He was never a God-fearing child, or man, in the grim Puritan phrase. Rather he put his hand in God's with love and perfect trust. His long hours of prayer were not a hardship or a duty, but a time of joyful communion and comfort.

If Brother André's secular learning was neglected, his spiritual tutorship was of the highest quality. While he was a child and thought as a child, his mother's gentle, simple faith fulfilled his needs perfectly. When he approached the age for his first Communion and had a need for greater understanding, he had the good fortune to find an inspired teacher.

Father André Provençal, the Curé of Saint Césaire, was one of those great men who serve the Lord in small ways. Of him, Bergeron says, "The Curé Provençal was a saint, father of all the world. He was a good papa adored by his parishioners. . . . When he walked down the street he carried his hat in his hand to avoid the necessity of constantly taking it off to salute everyone who greeted him. His progress through town was always *une fête*." On the monument they erected to his memory in Saint Césaire his people wrote the words: "He was good. He loved us."

Father Provençal lived in the cottage-like stone presbytery which snuggled up to his small fieldstone church. On the other side of his house was the three-story brick building of the convent school which he had founded and put in the hands of the Sisters of the Presentation in 1857, where 150 little girls from Saint Césaire and adjacent villages studied the three R's, as well as Latin and English. The cemetery behind the church and the meadows back of the convent ran down to the rounded, grassy banks of the slow-moving Yamaska River which curved affectionately around Saint Césaire. It was a serene sort of place.

Alfred Bessette spent most of his spare time either in the church or at the presbytery. Father Provençal made him welcome. Shortly after his mother's death, the Curé began to instruct Alfred for his first Communion. He had an eager pupil. The youth cared nothing for history or the current doings of the world—he probably never read a newspaper in his life—but he was avid to learn all there was to know about our Lord and His teachings. It so happened that Father Provençal particularly loved Saint Joseph. He communicated this devotion to his small pupil who was already so inclined. The Curé told Alfred how Saint Joseph had been declared the patron saint of Canada in 1624 by the Récollet Fathers, the first Catholic missionaries who came to Quebec. He described all that was known of Saint Joseph's life: his tender care of Mary and the Infant Jesus, his hard and humble life as a carpenter. "He is the model for all good workmen," Father Provençal declared.

Brother André remembered replying proudly, "My father was a carpenter, too."

The Nadeaus bought Alfred a fine blue suit for his first Communion, and had his picture taken in it by the local photographer. It shows a round-faced little boy with carefully brushed hair and snapping black eyes. He is wearing a properly serious expression, but one senses that he is ready to break into laughter the moment the photographer releases the bulb. All his life Brother André loved to laugh in spite of his intense preoccupation with spiritual things—even perhaps because of it. For he once remarked, "A religious who is sad is a sad religious."

I, the undersigned Curé of Saint-Césaire, certify . . . that Alfred Bessette was confirmed in the Church of Saint-Césaire on June 7, 1858 by Monseigneur J. C. Prince.

[37]

Did the Servant of God practice any penitences before his entry into the religious life?

To this question Madame Lafleur replied, "Already as a child he practiced penitences, sacrificing his leisure. He prayed so long that sometimes my mother was afraid he would injure his health."

Adélard Fabre testified: "The only detail I recall of the penitences of Brother André is the following: One day when I was cleaning Brother André's room at the Oratory I showed him a piece of leather with tacks sticking out of it. I thought it was some useless piece of harness, but Brother André said, 'Give me that!' and took it away from me.

"So I learned that Brother André used it as a belt beneath his soutane.

"I said to him, 'It is not sensible to wear a belt like that around your body.' Then he told me that when he was a young man he wore a far worse one. I did not see that belt again."

Though she died before she could testify in the Cause, Mme. Nadeau had told Father Bergeron the story of that other belt. One day when Alfred was quite ill she was helping him make his bed. She saw him grimace with pain and noticed a ridge under his clothing. "What are you wearing under your shirt?" she asked.

"Nothing," he said like any embarrassed little boy.

"Let me see it, child."

She lifted up his shirt and discovered the leather belt armed with tacks.

"You're going crazy," she said. "With bad health like yours, it's ridiculous to make such a penitence!"

Alfred shyly said, "It was a sacrifice I had promised. Forgive me! I won't wear it any more."

His aunt hugged and kissed him and took the belt away. A little later she had to take an iron chain away from him, and again he promised not to wear it again. But he always invented new sacrifices. His young cousins told on him, "Mother, Alfred doesn't sleep in his bed. He sleeps on the floor. We saw him, Mother, we saw him!"

Mme. Nadeau understood by Alfred's sheepish expression that it was true. "You'll make yourself sick," she said crossly. "Don't do it any more!"

Naturally such a boy was an easy target for his hearty cousins. Though they loved him, and he them, they simply could not resist teasing him. They never knew whether Alfred would laugh at the joke on himself or burst into tears. In the light of his later life, it is evident that these ordeals of Alfred's youth and the penitences he imposed on himself were a testing and a preparation. At the same time such a child must have been a trial to those who loved him. They could not understand him, or foresee the life for which he was preparing himself; nor could he. He did these things because something within him made him want to sacrifice himself for love of God.

Did the Servant of God practice his religion faithfully in his youth?

Father Albert Cousineau, Superior of Saint Joseph's during Brother André's last years, answered, "Brother André told me that never once had he neglected to say his Rosary. At one time he used to go to a stable where he spent hours on his knees praying and meditating before a crucifix."

That was after Timothée Nadeau had moved his family to Farnham, and Alfred went to work on M. Ouimet's farm. The Ouimets were not as religious as the Bessettes. They went to Mass on Sunday, but that was the extent of their devotion. Alfred found it difficult to understand them. In addition the hard work on the farm and the distance from town made it impossible for him to keep up his own devotions. He did not have a place of his own to pray.

Then he had a happy chance. Ouimet went to an auction. An

old wooden crucifix was knocked down to him for a few sous —he was a man who could not resist a bargain. When he brought it home, Alfred's eyes were so bright with pleasure that Ouimet could not help saying, "Would you like this for your own?"

"Oh so much, so very much!"

"Take it then," Ouimet said brusquely. "I don't need it."

Alfred clasped it, and thought of the one place where he could be quiet. He carried his treasure out to the barn and hung it on a nail. Then he knelt down on the straw in an ecstasy of happiness.

After that Alfred spent all his spare time in the barn. Rainy days were lucky days for him because he could remain there for hours kneeling before his crucifix. He formed the habit of carrying on long conversations with Saint Joseph. Not that he thought his patron saint answered him in words; but as he talked a sense of complete understanding and accord entered his soul.

The Road to
Notre-Dame-des-Neiges

When did the Servant of God first go to the United States?

In reply, Arthur Saint-Pierre, who wrote the earliest history of Saint Joseph's Oratory, replied: "I do not know exactly when or why Brother André went to the United States."

Other witnesses were equally vague about this particular period of Brother André's life. However, the researches of Father Bergeron turned up the essential facts.

For several years Alfred Bessette worked sporadically between bouts of illness on the farms around Farnham. He even tried to become a blacksmith—that was an unhappy experience. As he approached his twentieth birthday he realized that he was getting nowhere in life and probably would remain a failure as long as he stayed in that poverty-stricken countryside.

This feeling was shared by many French-Canadian farmers of the era. It was a time of agricultural depression and the marginal farms of the Richelieu Valley no longer afforded a man a decent living. At the same time, just below the Canadian Border things were booming. The American Civil War of 1861–65 had produced an era of tremendous prosperity in the New England states coupled with an acute shortage of manpower. There were jobs to be had for the asking at what seemed fantastically high wages to the *habitants*. Thousands of them left for this Eldorado, and some returned with pockets full of cash and tall tales of riches to be gained.

It is unlikely that financial inducements were the main reason for Alfred's decision to go to America—he never cared for money at all. More likely he felt himself to be a burden on his relatives and friends, and hoped to relieve them and gain self-respect. He talked the project over with Father Springer, the Curé of Farnham, for whom he often did odd chores. The Curé advised him to try it for the reason that the American climate was less severe and might be better for his health.

Father Bergeron advances a more mystical reason for Alfred's decision. He believes that young Bessette was inspired to go to the United States as further preparation for his life work. He says "The good God . . . led him to the United States . . . to render him more sympathetic to Americans and so to facilitate the expansion of the cult of Saint Joseph. Much later the work of Brother André spread itself as rapidly in the United States as in Canada."

One thing is certain. Alfred Bessette spent long hours on his knees talking to Saint Joseph before he made up his mind, and he must have felt that his "saint of predilection" approved; otherwise he would not have gone.

Picture him then as he started on his adventure. Though he was about twenty years old, he was so small and frail that he looked no more than fifteen or sixteen. His face was oddly square for his slight build, and his dark eyes were lively. He first went to Connecticut where a friend, whose name is known to history as Pierre, had a job waiting for him in a textile factory in Moosup.

For the next three years Alfred appears to have wandered around New England in what he himself described as a vagabond existence. His weak stomach could not long tolerate the exhausting work in the noisy, airless factories of that era—

twelve hours was an average working day. So he alternated between highly paid industrial jobs and less lucrative but healthier work on the farms. Beside Moosup he also lived in Hartford and Phoenix, towns which he revisited many times.

Only one noteworthy thing happened to him during those years, and it is well attested. Witness after witness swore before the Tribunal that Brother André had told them the story, each time in almost the same words.

He was working in a hayfield, so exhausted after an endless day that all he could think of was dying. He leaned on his rake and fell into one of his silent conversations with his great protector. "Where will I die, Saint Joseph?" he asked.

Brother André always described what followed, not as a vision, but a waking dream. In his mind's eye he saw a great stone, barracks-like building with many dormer windows and a tall spire surmounted by a cross. He had never seen this place before; nor could he have, for it was not yet built. Years later when he saw the new building of the College of Notre Dame in Côte-des-Neiges, where he was assigned by Holy Cross as doorman, he instantly recognized it as the place of his dream. However, he mistook the prophecy. He did not die at Notre Dame; but he lived there for forty years.

When did the Servant of God return from the United States, and what did he do then?

Arthur Saint-Pierre answered: "To my knowledge, Alfred Bessette went to live with relatives in the village of Sutton, close to the American border. I know that he frequently saw l'Abbé Provençal, Curé of Saint Césaire, and I know that it was on the advice of Father Provençal that Brother André requested admission in the Congregation of Holy Cross."

Alfred Bessette returned after three years in America no richer except in self-knowledge. He was still a partial pensioner of his relations, still a failure in a worldly sense. But he had recognized his vocation. He knew now that he was only really happy when he felt himself close to God and Mary and Saint Joseph. So completely was he imbued with love of God that all worldly things were mere interruptions to his all-pervasive passion. None of the strange or beautiful things he had seen in his travels interested him at all except as manifestations of God's goodness. Thus he came to the conclusion that the world was not for him.

The problem was how to leave it. With his lack of education, his inability even to read a letter, he believed that no religious order would accept him. He felt that the one person who might help him was the Curé of Saint Césaire. Throughout his stay in America he had corresponded with Father Provençal. He accomplished this by dictating his letters to a friend, who in turn read the Curé's letter to him. As soon as he was settled in Sutton, he started afoot for Saint Césaire, getting lifts on farm wagons.

He found one great change in the static little town. A college had sprung up across the street from the church and the convent. It was a yellow brick building seventy feet long with a steeply pitched roof surmounted by a belvedere topped by a cross. Alfred soon learned that this was another result of Father Provençal's interest in education. He had raised the money for it, and asked the Brothers of Holy Cross to staff it. It had just opened that November of 1869, with six brothers as teachers and eighty pupils ranging in age from eight to fourteen years old.

Otherwise Saint Césaire was just the same as when he had last been there. Best of all, Father Provençal had not changed at all. He sat in his great carved oak armchair with his bald, domelike head glistening in the light of an oil lamp and looked fondly at Alfred from beneath his heavy eyebrows.

In the light of the humbleness and timidity of his nature, one may imagine the trepidation with which Alfred explained his desire to devote himself to the service of God. His own words leave no doubt that he considered it presumptuous for him even to imagine that he would be considered worthy. Undoubtedly Father Provençal questioned him kindly but closely about his decision. In fact they had many such talks. It is evident that the Curé was greatly moved by these conversations with Bessette. Not that he was surprised, for after all he had watched the boy for over ten years now. He remembered that in the old days when he wanted to find Alfred to do some errand for him, the first place he looked was in the church, where he usually found the small, thin, little figure on its knees in wrapt devotion before the statue of Saint Joseph holding the Christ Child. Now he realized that the boy had grown to spiritual maturity. Later the Curé showed how deeply he was impressed by the spiritual qualities of this strangely wise, illiterate young man.

Given the understanding nature of Father Provençal it was inevitable that his advice would be that Alfred should become a religious.

"But who would have me?" was the next question.

One can almost see Father Provençal's affectionate smile as he answered in words that Brother André remembered, "It is not necessary to be a professor to become a religious. Many brothers work with their hands. Why don't you talk with our friends across the street?"

Naturally, Alfred Bessette knew nothing about the Congregation of Holy Cross, but he wanted desperately to learn. He stayed for some weeks in Saint Césaire, probably as Father Provençal's guest at the presbytery, earning his keep by doing chores around the church and spending as much time as he could with the brothers.

One may imagine that he was something of a nuisance to the six men who were trying to cope with organizing a brand new school and teaching and disciplining eighty rambunctious young boys. Brother André remembered that they were not enthusiastic about his aspirations. Being practical men they considered that such a frail recruit would be more of a liability than an asset to their community.

But being truly religious, which implies a large measure of love for humanity as well as love of God, they devoted as much time as possible to Alfred's avid questions. From them and Father Provençal he learned the whole history of Holy Cross. His mind, uncluttered by learning, retained it all.

In France, in 1820, the religious had been driven out of the country and there were not enough secular priests to attend to the spiritual needs of the people and teach the children. This state of affairs led l'Abbé Jacques François Dujarié, Curé of Ruillé-sur-Loire near Le Mans, to found an association designed to provide sacristans and schoolmasters to help the overworked priests. He named them the Brothers of Saint Joseph.

In 1835 l'Abbé Dujarié gave the authority over his group of brothers to Canon Basile Moreau, who had just founded an association of auxiliary priests. Two years later the Congregation of Holy Cross was formed when the members of the two associations came together in the District of Sainte-Croix, at Le Mans, from which they took their name.

Unlike such societies as the Jesuits in which the lay brothers have no say in governing the order, the priests and brothers of Holy Cross are separate entities under one general government. Each elects members of the General Council. A General Chapter is held every six years which elects the Superior General. All the members are constituted in the religious state by the simple vows of poverty, chastity and obedience. The vow of poverty means that a member of the order can possess nothing of his own, can accept no gifts and spend no money without the express permission of his superior. The vow of chastity is obvious. The vow of obedience means that he must obey the orders of his superior unless they contravene the moral law—if his superior orders him to commit murder he does not have to do it. If he refuses to obey a legitimate command it is a sin, though not always a mortal sin. However, if his superior says,

"In the name of your vow of obedience" or "in the name of our Lord, Jesus Christ," this is an official order and to disobey it is a mortal sin.

In Brother André's time, priests, teaching brothers and working brothers were all equal in Holy Cross. The Sacred Congregation of Propaganda in Rome, in approving its charter, called it, "An Institute composed of priests and lay brothers so well united that while conserving the nature of each of the two societies neither prevails over the other, but both work together in the best manner possible." Pope Pius IX decreed the approval of the Institute in 1857.

There is a charming tradition concerning the uniform of the order. When Canon Moreau went to see Pope Pius IX to gain his approval, the Holy Father asked, "What habit do you plan for the members of your congregation?"

Canon Moreau, slightly embarrassed, said, "I have not thought of that yet."

Whereupon the Pope said, smiling, "Why not adopt mine?"

For this reason the priests of Holy Cross wear over their soutanes short papal capes, only they are black instead of white like the Pope's. The lay brothers wear only the soutane with a medal of Saint Joseph instead of the priestly crucifix.

Long before they received papal approval the Religious of Holy Cross had spread half across the world. By 1841 they had established a foundation in Africa and one in Indiana which became the great University of Notre Dame. They came to Canada at the urgent request of Monseigneur Ignace Bourget, Bishop of Montreal. Led by Father Louis-Auguste Vérité, six lay brothers, one of whom was an architect, arrived on May 27, 1847, with $50 in cash. They established themselves in a small stone house in the parish of Saint Laurent in Montreal. Nearby was a large wooden building which could be converted into a school. These houses and some land were presented to Holy Cross by M. le Curé Germain. The new community set to work almost immediately. They took twelve boarding pupils in the stone house, and found a space six feet square at the back of the parlor which they made into a chapel. This became Saint Laurent College.

From this small beginning Holy Cross expanded slowly—the need for Catholic teachers in Quebec was very great, but there was very little money. However, by 1870, the year Brother André made his decision, the College of Saint Laurent had been greatly enlarged and two new institutions had been founded: the college at Saint Césaire, and a combined school for younger boys and a novitiate in the old Hotel Bellevue at Côte-des-Neiges on the western slope of Mount Royal.

When did the Servant of God enter the religious life?

Father Albert Cousineau, who was Superior General of Holy Cross, and is now Bishop of Cap Haitien, answered: "Brother André made his novitiate at the Côte-des-Neiges and later at Saint Laurent when the novitiate was transferred there. He took the holy habit on December 27, 1870."

Brother André's decision was not made hurriedly. For the better part of a year he meditated and prayed, making numerous visits to his friend and adviser in Saint Césaire. He was strongly attracted to Holy Cross because of his personal devotion to Saint Joseph to whom the order was dedicated. Indeed, at that time the brothers were still called the Josephites. In that same year, 1870, Pope Pius IX named Saint Joseph the Protector of the Universal Church.

It was not until October, 1870, that Father Provençal sat down to write a letter of recommendation for his young friend Alfred Bessette to Father Julien Gastineau, Superior of the pupils and Director of Novices at the Hotel Bellevue. The letter is a matter of record. In it he used a phrase which may have been more prophetic than he knew. The Curé of Saint Césaire wrote, "I send you a saint for your community."

With this letter, which of course he had not read, clutched

tightly in his hand, Alfred Bessette started on the long trip to Montreal. In mid-November he presented himself at the Hotel Bellevue. It was a rambling, white wooden structure with four columns supporting a portico in front. The planking of the old building was so loosely joined that a contemporary description says, "In times of storm the inhabitants did not know where to take refuge from being inundated." As Brother André knocked at the front door that November, the snow was already deep around it.

Father Gastineau received him warmly and put him to work at once—they were as usual short-handed. It was certainly no easy life, as the schedule of the community indicates. The pupils were awakened at five thirty in the morning—the brothers had to be up at five. Breakfast was at six thirty. From that time on, there was not a moment when everyone was not hard at work or at prayer until the final prayers, spiritual reading and bed at seven thirty. Then only could Alfred slip into the improvised chapel alone for his prayers and meditations.

Naturally, being the newest hand he got the dirtiest jobs. He spent most of the day on his knees scrubbing and cleaning, for the ramshackle old building was a glorious dirt-catcher. However, as Bergeron puts it, "Alfred was not, as so many young men are, drawn back by the pleasures of the world. Rather his heart was open to spiritual ideals. He was accustomed to the tenderness of Jesus toward those He loves as well as to the trials, the whip and the Cross which they share with Him."

After several weeks of proving his willingness to withstand the exigencies of the religious life and confirming his vocation by long hours of prayer, Alfred Bessette was accepted as a novice.

The simple ceremony in which the young postulant gives himself to God is always impressive. To Alfred Bessette it was transcendently joyful. A supreme moment for him was when the presiding priest said, "Alfred Bessette, from now on you will call yourself Brother André."

[51]

He had chosen to bear that name in religion as a witness to his gratitude to the Curé of Saint Césaire, Father André Provençal.

Was the Servant of God a faithful novice?

Again let Father Cousineau answer: "I know, by the oral tradition of the community, that Brother André was a faithful novice."

He was that. Indeed his one idea was to express in every action of his life the doctrine of Christ and the ideals of the Gospels, so far as a mortal may. He often despaired that he fell far short of this goal. When he became troubled he turned to Father Gastineau. The Superior was a very busy man whose face was stern, his eyebrows were creased in what appeared to be a perpetual frown. But his appearance belied his nature; occupied as he was, he spent many hours with his young charge counseling with spiritual wisdom and comforting the young man who had been recommended to him as a saint.

Halfway through his novitiate, in the autumn of 1871, Brother André was transferred to Saint Laurent. The college had grown beyond the ability of its small staff to cope with and the brothers sent a call for help from the novices on Côte-des-Neiges. Father Gastineau remained Superior of the school, and Father Guy became Director of Novices at Saint Laurent.

Brother André was quartered in the long whitewashed building, called the White House, which had been the original school of Holy Cross in Canada. He was given three tasks: to mend the clothes of the other brothers and priests, to nurse the sick and to keep the main corridor clean.

Saint Laurent, with its hustle and confusion of students and the desperate efforts of an inadequate staff to meet the demands on them, was not an ideal place of preparation for a religious life. However, Brother André had the good fortune to find another splendid adviser to direct his spiritual life—he was not so lucky later. Father Hupier was a man of gentle wisdom. Indeed, Brother André regarded him with such reverence that after the priest died, he said, "Father Hupier appeared to me in a dream and said, 'Our Father' three times. Then he said to me, 'Often repeat those words, "Thy will be done." ' From that I knew that there would be many difficult ordeals in my life. How I pray that he may be in heaven!"

During his novitiate Brother André's main trouble continued to be his miserable health; apart from that he was very gay. But no matter how ardent his spirit, his stomach often betrayed him. During these spells of sickness he sometimes coughed up blood. Though the authorities knew how willing he was they decided that his strength was not equal to his zeal. Like the brothers at Saint Césaire, they feared he would be a liability to his community.

Extract from the minutes of the Provincial Council of the Congregation of Holy Cross, on the 8th of January, 1872:

> The brother André is not admitted to temporary vows because the state of his health gives no hope that he can be admitted to the profession.
>
> [signed]
> J. GASTINEAU—JOS. RÉZÉ
> J. C. ETHIER—FRÈRE AGATHON

This was undoubtedly the greatest ordeal Brother André ever faced—he called it *"une grande épreuve."* Sister Leblanc of the Sisters of Providence of Montreal testified before the Tribunal that fifty years later Brother André described it to her with great emotion. He was utterly crushed when the news was told him; so desperate, indeed, that for once he lost his timidity of people in high places.

Bishop Bourget, he who had brought Holy Cross to Canada, went one day to visit the College of Saint Laurent. He was by then in his seventies, but still active, with a thin noble face surmounted by rumpled silvery white hair. For a few moments the Bishop was left alone in the reception room. To his amazement the door suddenly flew open and a pale, shaking novice with an expression of agony on his face burst in.

Brother André described the scene to Sister Leblanc: "Monseigneur Bourget looked at me with great kindness and said, 'What do you want, my son?'

"I knelt at his feet and rested my clasped hands on his knees, looking up at him with great confidence. Monseigneur Bourget talked to me like a father."

The Bishop was deeply moved as the young novice told of his great love of God and his sorrow when his dream of becoming a religious was broken by his wretched health. With tears in his eyes he said, "My only ambition is to serve God in the most obscure tasks."

It would have taken a monster to refuse that plea. One may imagine that the Bishop himself was close to tears as he said, "Don't be afraid, child. You will be admitted to the religious profession."

Brother André's gratitude to the Bishop was as great as one would expect. After Bourget died, Brother André often said, "You must know what a high place he has in heaven!"

Coincidentally, he more than repaid his debt to the Bishop. Bourget died without achieving the great ambition of his life which he expressed in this letter:

> There should be a church dedicated to St. Joseph in memory of all his services to others, in which every day he would receive the public honors due to his eminent virtues. . . . We wish to consecrate all our strength and life to make that church a place of pilgrimage where one may come to visit him. . . .

The great Basilica of Saint Joseph of Mount Royal to which three million pilgrims come every year to venerate the husband of Mary was built by the inspiration and devotion of Brother André.

The following document now appears in the record of the Tribunal:

August 22, 1872

In the name of the Father and of the Son and of the Holy Ghost, Amen.

I, Brother André, called in the world Alfred Bessette, all unworthy as I am, led nevertheless by the desire to serve the adorable Trinity, I make for one year to Almighty God the vows of poverty, chastity and obedience, in the sense of the laws and constitutions of this congregation, in the presence of Our Lord Jesus Christ, of the Blessed Virgin Mary, conceived without sin, of her worthy husband Saint Joseph, and of all the Heavenly Court, promising to accept whatever employment which it pleases my superiors to confide to me.

Signed: Frère André, called in the world Alfred Bessette, in the Chapel of the College of Notre Dame, Côte-des-Neiges.

So Brother André was permitted to take the temporary vows which were one more step toward his ultimate ambition of "serving God in the most obscure tasks." He was able to sign the document because he had learned to read and write, though with some difficulty, during his novitiate.

For eighteen months more he continued to serve his apprenticeship to God. During this time he wrote a happy letter to the Nadeaus. It is one of only two letters he is known to have written:

DEAR UNCLE AND DEAR AUNT:

I find myself happy in the state I have embraced, without, however, forgetting my benefactors. . . . Dear Uncle, if I have too long deferred responding to your kind letter it is because I wished to wait until the fete of your glorious patron [saint].

Since it is the general custom among families to present a bouquet on the fete day of the father, what bouquet more precious and more perfumed could I present to you on this day than the memory of your kindnesses to me! What richer bouquet could I present you than the memory of all the pains and all the cares that you gave yourself for me?

Finally, the record shows that on February 21, 1874, "after all the formalities required by the laws and constitutions, Brother André . . . made his religious profession at the hands of the Very Reverend Father Lefebvre, Superior Provincial, in the Chapel of Notre-Dame-du-Sacré-Coeur, Côte-des-Neiges."

There is a formal photograph of Brother André taken for this occasion. He is wearing a brand new soutane with a black silk cincture and heavy fringed tassels. One hand is holding a Bible upright on a small table. Though he was nearly thirty he looks so appealingly young that he might almost be a new acolyte with a proud, intense look on his square, earnest face.

Brother André had no doubt whatever that his happiness was due to Bishop Bourget's intervention. Indeed, to the very end, the Superior of Novices, Father Guy, had serious doubts, though he was sympathetically inclined toward the new brother. When he finally accepted him he wrote, almost apologetically, "If this young man becomes incapable of working, at least he will know how to pray very well."

The Door

W*hat employment was assigned to the Servant of God after he made his profession?*

Father Cousineau testified: "After his profession, I know that the Servant of God filled the function of porter at the College of Notre-Dame-du-Sacré-Coeur in Côtes-des-Neiges.

"It is reported that Brother André used to say, 'On my entrance into the community they showed me the door and I remained there for forty years.'"

At first Brother André worked at the Hotel Bellevue, where he had started his novitiate. But the school was growing fast and the funds of Holy Cross were increasing. To accommodate the pupils the congregation decided to build a large college on what is now Queen Mary Road facing the forested western slope of Mount Royal. It was as modern as the Hotel Bellevue was primitive. Capable of accommodating two hundred pupils it had the last word in central heating and "water and gas arrived there through iron conduits while the appliances were as good as those in the greatest institutions." As Brother André watched the façade of cut stone being built and saw the slender spire set in place it was as though he were watching the mansion of his daydream in America rising before his eyes.

The college was ready for occupancy in the autumn of 1881.

The whole establishment was then transferred from the Hotel Bellevue. Brother André moved into the little porter's cell, which he occupied for almost forty years.

Since his presence there eventually made it the most famous porter's lodge in North America, one should observe it closely. It was a true cell, long and very narrow with a disproportionately high ceiling. The trim was dark brown varnished wood and the walls were bare white plaster. Brother André decorated them with a small wooden crucifix and his little statue of Saint Joseph before which burned a lamp "nourished by olive oil." One tall narrow window looked out across a potato field at the steep, densely wooded side of Mount Royal. Brother André used to stand there looking up at the rugged crest and meditating on what a wonderful place it would be for a shrine to Saint Joseph.

The furniture of the cell consisted of a small wardrobe, a wooden chair, and a fat little roll-top desk on a chest of drawers. Along one wall was a cushioned bench less than a foot wide with a pillow at one end where the porter could perhaps snatch at a few moments sleep between midnight and Matins.

For this porter's job entailed a great deal more than opening the front door to visitors. The college was chronically under-manned and every member of the staff worked at a dead run. Brother André was given a multitude of tasks. It was he who rang Matins at five o'clock in the morning, then knocked on every door saying, *"Benedicamus Domino."* After morning devotions and breakfast he cleaned the reception room and three long corridors. He also ran errands to town, and at noon went to the post office for the mail. Every Monday he took the pupils' dirty laundry in a carriage to their respective homes and picked it up on Saturdays. In his spare time he was the barber for all two hundred boys. They paid him fifteen sous a haircut with his Superior's permission, and he carefully put the money in a little box for a purpose that was hardly formulated in his mind.

Another duty was making the twisted, tasseled cinctures for

the brothers. He had a hard time with the tassels at first—they were badly designed. So he carved one out of wood, and covered it with cloth and fringe. This was the standard tassel of the Community for years.

And all day long and part of the night he was answering the bell, and going to find the members of the staff whom visitors or pupils wished to see. One pictures the eager little brother— he was hardly more than five feet tall—scampering madly through the corridors with his soutane and tassels flying as he searched breathlessly for the desired person.

M. Pichette testified: "Brother André also helped the youngest children to get dressed and often took them for a walk. The children loved to go out with him. . . . He told me that he had never lost a child en route.

"At night when he retired to his room," M. Pichette continued, "he used to repair his vestments. He did the same for his trousers and his slippers. As to his underclothes, he did not repair them for the good reason, as he told me, that he almost never wore any.

"He avowed to me that often he had no more than thrown himself on his bed, when already the hour of rising had come."

In spite of his zeal, Brother André was often in trouble those days. In 1880 his beloved Father Gastineau had been replaced as Superior by Father Auguste Louage. Father Louage was stormy by nature. He had a pudgy face, prominent eyes and a very short temper. In truth his work of running the college was enough to make a man irascible, what with obstreperous children, demanding parents and an overworked staff. For some reason the little porter seemed to get on his nerves and he eased his tensions by constantly scolding him. The other religious used to call Brother André "the lightning rod of the college because he receives the bolts of Louage."

Of this Brother Osée Coderre, C.S.C., testified: "Brother André certainly had his ordeals. I remember one time when he had gone as usual to get the mail. I had replaced him at the door that morning at his request. I left my post for a few moments and during that time someone rang the bell. The Father Provincial, the Reverend Father Louage, descended from the second floor to answer the door. At that moment Brother André returned with the mail. The Father Provincial angrily asked, 'Where were you, Brother André?'

"The latter replied, 'I went to the post office.'

"The Father Provincial said: 'Look! I am Provincial, Superior, and Bursar. And now it seems I must be porter also. Very well, Brother André, kiss the floor!'

"Brother André obeyed without a word."

Brother André never mentioned this incident, probably because he thought no more about it. He took his vow of obedience very seriously, and if his Superior ordered him to kiss the floor, kiss it he would. However, in view of his sense of humor it is quite possible that his eyes twinkled as he did so.

He tried all the harder to please Father Louage. One day he heard the Superior say he wished there were a parterre in front of the college. Brother André said, "Very late in the evenings I carried away many rocks which I removed from the land each day in the short intervals between my different occupations. An amusing thing—I used two wheelbarrows to save time. I would push one a hundred yards and walk back to get the other, resting myself and reciting my Rosary. Several times while I was still working, the cocks' crowing reminded me that it was time to ring the awakening bell."

It was during this time that Brother André formed the habit of eating alone. When the Cause went to Rome, the devil's advocate objected that the Servant of God did not live a good communal life in that he seldom ate with his confreres.

This was true. When the others were at meals, Brother André had to stay at the door. So he took his meals on his desk in the porter's cell. Because his stomach still troubled him, his meals almost always consisted of a bowl of milk, watered down, in which he soaked a few pieces of bread.

Brother André told many witnesses that he could not digest the food at the communal table. But when one of the brothers suggested that he ask for specially digestible food he replied, "I will not do that, for it might hurt the cook's feelings."

Did the Servant of God observe his religious duties at Notre Dame?

Brother Osée replied: "During his life Brother André had the reputation among his confreres of being a very good religious."

And Father Cousineau testified: "I can say that Brother André faithfully kept his obligation to our Lord, to the Holy Sacrament and to the Sacred Heart. He observed equally faithfully the Commandments of God and of the Church. He assisted regularly at Mass on Sunday and holy days of obligation, confessed frequently, received Communion every morning and fasted on Friday. Furthermore he fasted practically all his life, all the days."

With his multifarious duties Brother André worried that he had too little opportunity for religious exercises. He was forever trying to steal some time for prayer. In the morning after communal prayers when the others had gone he would remain in the chapel while the priest said Mass, kneeling on the pavement at the back near the door so he could run and answer his bell if it rang.

Often he would beg a fellow religious to take the door for "fifteen minutes" while he went to the chapel. There he would kneel meditating on the sufferings of the Savior or talking with Saint Joseph. One of his confreres told of an occasion when he impatiently waited for Brother André to come back to his post. Finally he went into the chapel where he found the porter kneeling happily at the entrance to the choir. "Brother André," he said crossly, "you have been at prayer for two hours. Surely that's enough!"

Brother André, looking completely bemused, said, "Oh—is it that long? Please let me have five minutes more!"

Brother André found that the best time to pray was late at night when all the community were in bed. There in the darkened nave, lit only by the wine-red glow of the oil lamps burning before the sacred statues and the flickering votive candles, he would often pray the night away. On Wednesdays and Saturdays which were the days he washed the floor of the parlor, he was especially tired. Once he asked a young priest to come to the chapel with him, "to wake me if I fall asleep at my prayers."

The priest, much edified agreed, but Brother André's prayers lasted so long that the weary priest told his colleagues, "I'll never do that again!"

He also continued the penitences he had begun as a child, wearing an iron chain under his clothes. Late in his life he confided that, "Often during the winter nights I would throw a pitcher of cold water over myself, or go out in a somber corner of the yard back of the college and roll naked in the snow."

Brother André said that he practiced these mortifications to subdue the temptations of the devil. In fact, like many another holy man, he fought a running battle with the devil all his life, as witnesses to some of his encounters with Satan will presently testify.

Of course these rigors, long days of incessant work and nights of prayer, played havoc with Brother André's health. One Sunday after an all-night session he looked so bad that even a little boy could notice it. One of the pupils said anxiously, "Brother André, how you have changed since yesterday!"

The little brother grinned at him and said, "I am always careful to change every Sunday."

If the pupils noticed his unhealthy appearance his colleagues were seriously worried. They made him consult the college doctor, who said that he must do no more hard work for a while.

The next day, a Wednesday, the physician found him down on his knees washing the parlor floor. Brother André smiled up at the doctor's horrified expression and said, "If I die, the community will be disembarrassed of me."

Then his colleagues thought of another plan to make him rest. They decided to lock the chapel up at night. They tell the story—this is not sworn testimony, but it was believed in the community—that Brother André opened the door, never noticing that it was locked.

De Miraculis

What events first brought special fame of sanctity to the Servant of God?

Father Cousineau: "After his novitiate, when he was porter at the College of Notre Dame, Brother André made himself noticed by his devotion to Saint Joseph. One fact first attracted attention. Brother Aldéric suffered from a running wound on his leg. At the suggestion of Brother André he made a novena in honor of Saint Joseph, and on the morning of the nineteenth of March [the Fete of Saint Joseph], Brother Aldéric was cured.

"A second case which shows the influence of Brother André: a pupil of the College of Notre Dame was taken with a malignant fever according to the testimony of the college physician. Brother André saw the child and said to him, 'You have no more fever. You can go out and play.' Which the child did."

So in his carefully factual, colorless way Father Cousineau described the first of those extraordinary happenings at Notre Dame which many believe to be the earliest manifestations of Saint Joseph's love for Brother André, and which led to such great events.

Long afterward Brother André himself told the story of the sick child, and it was confirmed by many people who remembered it.

One of the pupils had been in the infirmary for several days with a malignant fever. At recess time Brother André went to see the lonely little boy. "What are you doing lying lazily here?" he asked.

"I'm sick," the child answered.

"Get up!"

"The doctor won't let me."

"You're not sick. Go out and play."

Feeling fine the boy dressed and rushed gaily out to join his friends.

What a row that caused! Doctor Charette came storming at Brother André, accusing him of meddling in the management of the infirmary and of grave imprudence.

"But the child is not sick," Brother André said. "Go and examine him."

The doctor called the boy in; took his temperature and made a thorough examination. He could find nothing wrong. Completely baffled, he examined the child at least three more times that day. Finally he attested to the permanence of the cure.

Other remarkable things happened to which Father Cousineau could testify. Not that he was present at the time, but having lived in the community so long he had been told these things by his older confreres, who, he knew, were truthful men.

There was, for example, the time when an epidemic of smallpox broke out at the College of Saint Laurent. The White House, which was now the infirmary, was filled to overflowing with sick students and religious. Many of them died. Father Beaudet, Superior of the college, sent to Notre Dame for help to nurse the sick who were in quarantine. Brother André joyfully responded in spite of warnings that his weak constitution made him vulnerable to the disease.

Now the accounts of what happened differ slightly. According to one, as Brother André entered the chapel at Saint Laurent he fell on his knees and prayed for the intercession of Saint Joseph to stop the plague. Brother Osée's account states that

Brother André organized a procession with the statue of Saint Joseph at its head which visited all the rooms of the college. Most likely he did both.

But on one thing all the records agree. From the day Brother André came to the college, the epidemic diminished rapidly and there were no more deaths.

As to another of these first signs of divine favor, let Father Cousineau testify (remembering that he, like all the witnesses, is speaking under the obligation of that sacred oath):

"Another extraordinary fact occurred in 1884, of which Brother Emery, who is still living, was a witness. A woman who was suffering from rheumatism was brought to see Brother André, who at that moment was occupied in brushing the floor. They told him of her trouble. Brother André contented himself by saying, 'Let her walk!'

"When the woman and her companions insisted that Brother André pay more attention, he addressed her directly, at the same time continuing to work, 'You are not sick any more. You can go home.'

"That woman went home cured."

In addition to these major events other things happened which are difficult to explain. For example, it was the custom of the brothers to go to houses where a death had occurred to prepare the body for burial. Many of the poor people had no money to pay an undertaker and some of the devout wanted none but sanctified hands to touch their dead. Brother André, like the other religious, often performed this unpleasant task, both as a charity and a form of penitence. According to the testimony of M. Pichette:

"A man who lived in Côte-des-Neiges died. This man had previously asked Brother André, whom he loved greatly, to take care of his body if he was the first to die. After his death, which occurred in the morning, the man's wife sent her child to ask Brother André to come and prepare the body. Brother André sent word that he was very busy and would come that evening. The wife sent the child back with the message that by evening it would be too late (because of rigor mortis). Brother André said to him, 'Reassure your mother, there will still be time this evening.'

"He went to the house about five o'clock. The wife had placed the body on a big white sheet. Brother André proceeded to make the toilette of the corpse and when he took it in his arms he saw the head change position. He straightened it, and noticed that the body had just begun to stiffen. And Brother André added, 'I believe he waited for me to lay him out because when I began his toilette, he was as though he had just that moment died.'"

According to Pichette's testimony, Brother André usually had *une nuit blanche* (a sleepless night) after laying out a corpse. He heard strange sounds and the objects on his table rattled around. Frequently he saw a large black cat which seemed to be responsible for the disturbance. He had his own explanation of this phenomenon. When one of his confreres in whom he had confided about the cat asked, "What do you think it is?" Brother André answered cheerfully, "The devil does not like me to do these good works. He is trying to frighten me."

Inevitably word of these wonders at Notre Dame filtered through its walls to the world outside. The schoolboys, who adored their barber, talked about him in their families and told how, if they felt sick or had a headache, a touch of his gentle little hands made it go away. Always when they thanked him, he said, "Don't thank me. It is Saint Joseph you must thank. Go and say a prayer to him."

Sick people began coming to Notre Dame to ring the bell and hope for a word or the touch of Brother André's hand. Quite often they went away healed. It was at this time that he began the practice to which he adhered throughout his life. He would give the sick person a medal of Saint Joseph. Then he would take a little of the oil from the lamp which burned before Saint Joseph's statue and rub the injured leg or the diseased chest with it, *outside the person's clothing*.

Once, late in his life, a skeptical friend asked Brother André if he thought the medal and the oil had any magical therapeutic value. Brother André smiled at his simplicity. "The medal is only metal," he said, "and the oil is just olive oil. But it makes them think more about Saint Joseph and so strengthens their faith."

As the cures multiplied so did the number of people coming to Notre Dame to see the little brother. In the midst of his many duties he always found time to rub them with Saint Joseph's oil and advise them to pray to the saint. Many were relieved of their sicknesses. Because of this Brother André got into trouble again.

Father Cousineau testified about it: "The number of the unhappy ones increased so greatly that the parents of the pupils, the confreres and the authorities of the college became upset. The parents feared contagion for their children. Among the confreres some said that it [Brother André's work] was folly, pride and illusion. Others declared that there was nothing wrong in letting the brother spread the devotion to Saint Joseph and it would be better to wait awhile before forbidding him to receive the sick."

The two schools of thought had some heated debates within the confines of the college. According to Brother Osée's testimony, "Brother Henri joined with Dr. Charette in twitting Brother André on the subject. Brother André suffered in silence and continued to rub the sick. In general the doctors were disquieted."

In a future that would have been utterly incredible to Brother André, the Promoter General of the Faith, in Rome, suggested that this testimony was adverse to his fame for sanctity. He spoke of the authorities' fear of Brother André bringing discredit on the college, and quoted the phrase "Folly, pride and illusion."

[71]

These were indeed severe ordeals for the little brother. But neither the fame which began to come to him—people already spoke of the saint at Notre Dame—nor the ordeals caused by skeptical doctors, nervous confreres, and the complaints of parents changed Brother André's course at all. He believed that the marvelous cures came from God and nothing made him so furious as to have them attributed to him. Azarias Claude testified that Brother André said to him, "How stupid people are to think that Brother André makes miracles. The good God makes the miracles, Saint Joseph obtains them. I am only the wire which transmits their blessings."

As to the sneering remarks some of his own confreres made about his methods, he regarded them simply as ordeals decreed by the Will of God and, suffering silently, went right on curing people. For the timid little brother was extremely stubborn when he felt that he was following the wishes of his patron saint.

This determination of his was particularly directed toward one great project which in those years of the 1880's seemed utterly impossible of accomplishment. In his rare moments of leisure Brother André continued to stare out of his narrow window at the tangled, towering wilderness of Mount Royal, and as he looked the idea that Saint Joseph must some day have a shrine there became more than a belief; it became an inspired conviction. In the testimony of the Cause there is an account of one of the brothers saying to the porter, "This is a strange thing. I place the statue of Saint Joseph in my cell facing my bed, and every time I come back someone has turned it around so it faces the mountain."

Brother André laughed. "It is not strange at all," he said, "it simply means that Saint Joseph wants to be honored on the mountain."

With that inspired purpose in his soul the timid little brother expected to accomplish the impossible.

The Shrine on the Mountain

THURSDAY was a half-holiday for the students of Notre Dame. On this day Brother André would sometimes find time to walk across the fields and orchards, and up a narrow little path in the forest to a cliff that projected like a cape beyond the trees. There he would stand meditating while he looked at the superb view of fields and farms and the church steeples of the villages in the Canadian plain. To the south he could see the blue shimmer of water where the Saint Lawrence River widened into Lake Saint Louis; while to west and north his eyes might follow the serpentine Rivière-des-Prairies embracing the Ile Jésus. The Two Mountains sprang abruptly from the plain like Mount Saint Grégoire of his youthful memory; and at the northernmost limit of vision were the hazy, violet waves of the Laurentian Mountains. It was, Brother André felt, the most fitting spot for a shrine to the patron saint of Canada. But it belonged to a farmer named Michel Guérin.

The official history of Notre Dame says that on a certain Thursday afternoon in 1890, one of the pupils, a little boy of ten, asked Brother André to take him along on his afternoon walk. Hand in hand they climbed the steep path. When they reached the projecting cape Brother André asked his small friend to kneel with him by a great tree. "I have hidden a medal of Saint Joseph here," he said. "We will pray that he will arrange the purchase of this land for us."

The little boy remembered that, when the prayer was finished, Brother André said again and again, "We will get this land. Saint Joseph must have a place!"

One may now trace the workings of faith through apparently unrelated events. In that year, 1890, Father Louis Geoffrion, who was now Superior of the college, became troubled about the situation of Notre Dame. A sporting club had opened up next door. People used to ski over the mountain from Montreal in winter to have a drink there; or ride out in the open trolley cars on summer evenings. There was talk of building other amusement places on the potato field across the road and the vacant land on the mountainside. Father Geoffrion pictured his beloved college in the center of satanic revelry. He very much wanted to buy that land. However, M. Guérin would not sell.

Brother André continued to pray on his mountain for six years. On one occasion Father Geoffrion went there with Brother Aldéric to place another medal in the tree and pray to Saint Joseph.

In 1896, M. Guérin's heart was finally softened and the sale went through. Holy Cross acquired about twenty-five acres of the mountainside, including the crest and Brother André's promontory. When the deed was signed, on July 22, 1896, the Religious of Saint-Croix went to work on their mountain. With Brother André working hardest of all they cleared and widened the path, cutting steps in the rocks where it was steepest. They also cleared an open space on the plateau. Then in procession they climbed the new trail. Brother André carried a statuette of Saint Joseph holding the Christ Child, which he placed in a little cave in the rocks. Others had a bucket of white paint. Triumphantly they painted in big letters on a rock the words: "BOULEVARD SAINT JOSEPH."

The first building, erected on the mountain in 1897, was a

little wooden belvedere or summerhouse. The official record in a suddenly lyric mood describes it "perched coquettishly on the plateau." It became a favorite picnic ground for the pupils, and a place of meditation for the Community of Holy Cross.

In the springtime of 1898, as part of the celebration of the fiftieth anniversary of Holy Cross in Canada, a little stage was built on the picnic grounds. In that theater whose scenery consisted of the leaves and flowers of the forest, the small pupils gave a charming play depicting the arrival of the Religious of Holy Cross. It was a happy day for Brother André. But he had a greater ambition for Saint Joseph.

It was also in 1898 that Brother André put a little bowl at the foot of his statuette of Saint Joseph on the hillside, hoping pilgrims would put offerings into it. When people came to see him in the parlor or the college he would suggest that they go up to the belvedere to enjoy the beautiful view. "And don't forget to say a prayer to Saint Joseph!"

Almost every evening now, he went up the hill to pray, and to see how much money was in the bowl. As he counted the pennies and nickels he would say gleefully, "Fifty cents today, for Saint Joseph."

In accordance with the rules of the community he had obtained the permission of the new Superior, Father Benjamin Lecavalier, to save the money to build a little shrine on the mountain. His hoard grew slowly, for his friends, though devout, were very poor. Six years passed before he accumulated the sum of two hundred dollars, which Father Lecavalier decided was sufficient for a beginning. The Superior, a handsome, straight-nosed man with a pompadour of silver hair, was sympathetic to Brother André. He obtained permission from Archbishop Paul Bruchési of Montreal for the little porter to build his shrine, and assigned Brother Abundius to the work. It was September, 1904, and Brother André had served as porter for almost thirty years.

From the testimony of Joseph Piché, in religion Brother Abundius, C.S.C.:

"I worked on the first chapel, I don't remember the exact year. Father Benjamin Lecavalier . . . was Superior at that time. I was the handyman at the college. The Superior asked me to build a chapel. I built it sixteen feet by twelve. The altar had to be made of pine. He [Brother André] had received a present from M. Dufresne, the sculptor, who had given the decorations for the interior of the tabernacle and certain pieces of wood. . . . Brother André was very hard-working. I heard Father Lecavalier say that he had never seen him so impatient. I think Brother André was ready for his mission. . . . The construction took about seven or eight days of my free time. Brother André was convinced that the chapel would have to be enlarged, but he was content that a start had been made."

One can picture the little brother hopping about in his impatience; trying very hard to help Brother Abundius and getting in the way of that competent carpenter, who said, "He did not do much good."

Many people have spoken of the naïve charm of that first minuscule chapel. It was so tiny that only the priests offering the Mass could be inside. Big double doors opened the whole back of it, and the congregation sat on ranks of backless benches up the mountainside which formed a natural amphitheatre. It had not even any windows; light came through a double ribbon of unpolished glass set in the sloping roof.

When the shrine was finished, there was still work to be done building a retaining wall of rocks to keep the ground from slipping down the steep slope, and widening Saint Joseph's Boulevard for the dignitaries and pilgrims who would come to the inauguration of the Oratory.

Brother André himself told how he got help in these tasks: "A man came to see me at the college. He was so thin that you felt you could see daylight through him. He had cancer of the stomach. I asked him, 'Could you come and work for me to-morrow morning?'

" 'I would like nothing better,' he said, 'but I have not the strength. I would have to be able to eat something.'

" 'Good,' I said, 'you will come to breakfast with me to-morrow.'

"The next day I gave him a good repast. He went to work the same day. All trace of his malady had disappeared. I employed him for several months."

Meanwhile Brother André had bought a beautiful old statue of Saint Joseph holding the Child. He induced one of the pensioners at the Home for the Aged to paint it in white and gold. The unknown sculptor had been inspired to depict in the serene bearded face of the Patriarch the infinite tenderness and love he felt for the Infant Jesus.

Brother André's first great moment—perhaps it was his greatest—came on October 19, 1904. That day Vicar General Monseigneur Z. Racicot came to preside at the inauguration of the new sanctuary. The ceremonies began in the chapel at Notre Dame, where Brother André had prayed so fervently for this favor. There the Vicar General blessed the statue of Saint Joseph. From there it was carried in triumph by four of the brothers. The Church dignitaries led the way and the statue was followed by the young students and their professors. The procession wound up the path through the bare trees, dripping from an autumnal drizzle, shrill voices and deep singing hymns in honor of Saint Joseph. When they reached the shrine, the statue was placed on the provisional altar. Then the people took their places on the benches in the rain "as though it were full summer." The Vicar General, assisted by Father Lecavalier, who was now Superior of Notre Dame, and Father Geoffrion, blessed the new chapel and spoke touchingly of the goodness of Saint Joseph.

After the Mass, Monseigneur Racicot blessed a smaller statue of the Patriarch which was hoisted to a niche over the door. So "the heavenly Protector of the Church reigned gloriously in his picturesque corner of the mountain. His statue on its dominating height above the main road would henceforth be saluted by thousands of Catholic travelers who came to Montreal."

And what of Brother André at his moment of triumph? As always when the great prelates of the Church, whom he respected so deeply, were present, he made himself as invisible as possible. But his humility did not dim his joy and pride, for these emotions were for Saint Joseph, not for himself.

So he stands a little apart in the rain, a tiny figure with curly white hair. He is almost sixty years old, having served God for thirty-four of those years. Yet with that prevision which is one of the favors accorded him, he knows that he stands at the very beginning of his life's work.

During the rigors of a Canadian winter the chapel could not be used publicly. However, Brother André lighted a lamp before the statue of the Patriarch, which burned night and day, and he, or one of his confreres, went there almost daily to render homage to Saint Joseph. In the spring a benefactor, who still remains anonymous, gave a Way of the Cross, which was erected canonically by Father P. Théophile, a Franciscan. On June 1, 1905, the Fete of the Ascension was celebrated at the Oratory for the first time. Mass was said before a considerable group of the faithful.

In August, Father Henri Rhault of the Parish of Saint Laurent, accompanied by most of his parishioners, celebrated Mass in the chapel on the mountain. The faithful were unlucky that day. A terrific thunderstorm broke just as Father Rhault finished his sermon, and the dripping congregation broke and ran for home.

Nevertheless, more and more pilgrims came to the Oratory, and Brother André's fund for enlarging the chapel to provide shelter for the faithful grew. Much of the money was provided by his friends the firemen. There was a fire station back of the college where he often went to chat with the men on duty. They became devoted to him, and their successors of today, the firemen of Montreal, still go to the basilica every Wednesday to help the hundreds of sick pilgrims who come that day to pray to be healed.

In the winter of 1906, Brother Abundius built a beautiful new altar. That spring the Fete of the Ascension was again celebrated at the Oratory. According to the newspaper *La Presse,* "it was an imposing religious ceremony. . . . The temperature was superb and the attendance numerous and diversified."

That year Father Georges A. Dion, who was Superior Provincial of Holy Cross, took up residence at Notre Dame and became Superior of the institution. He was a strong, stocky man with a high broad brow and kindly eyes, but a most determined chin. As Provincial, he of course knew about Brother André, and was prejudiced against him. In fact he was one of those who regarded the little brother with considerable reserve. In a year or two Brother André won him over completely, and the Superior supported him faithfully in one of his greatest ordeals. But at first he made matters very difficult.

On one of his first days in office as Superior of the College of Notre Dame, Father Dion went to inspect the Oratory. He saw a few crutches and braces, donated by those who had been cured, standing against the wall. "Take those things away," he said. "We do not want to be accused of superstition."

But Brother André pleaded so effectively, supported by witnesses to the cures, that Father Dion withdrew his order.

However, he imposed severe discipline on Brother André and opposed the enlargement of the Oratory.

In this regard, hear the testimony of Brother Osée in which he provides the first clue to Brother André's grand design:

"When Brother André desired to improve the road to the little chapel . . . he asked his Provincial, the good Father Dion, for authorization to spend on the road $300, which had been given him for the chapel. The Father Provincial showed himself to be unfavorable to the project, but ended by giving in to Brother André.

"A little later Brother André brought him another $500, and asked permission to spend it on the chapel. Whereupon the Father Provincial demanded of him, 'But what is this? Do you want to build a basilica up there?'

"Brother André just nodded his head. . . ."

As time went on and the alms of the pilgrims accumulated, Brother André finally got his way. To preserve the wooden building, its exterior walls were covered with sheet iron painted white as are the wooden houses of the *habitants* in the back country of his youth. The inside was also paneled in sheet iron of a *repoussé* design which was painted a pale, delicate green.

At the same time Father Dion allowed Brother André to present a petition to Archbishop Bruchési that the shrine be enlarged by building a nave, or at least a shed, to shelter the congregation. The Archbishop refused on the reasonable grounds that such a church might become a charge on the archdiocese which it could ill afford. Brother André was bitterly disappointed, but he prayed all the harder.

It was about this time that Brother André paid a brief visit to Saint Césaire, which resulted in a charming incident described in the official Summation of the Cause:

"A little boy five or six years old, the son of Liguori Berthiaume, limped up to Brother André using one crutch. "Will you cure me, Brother André?" he asked with great confidence.

With a twinkle Brother André said, "Go ask permission of your mamma to be cured."

Forgetting his crutch the child *ran* to ask his mother.

Such happy incidents atoned for the troubles of the time. In addition to the refusal of the Archbishop to permit enlarging the chapel, Father Dion had forbidden Brother André to receive the sick in the parlor of the college during visiting hours. He would not even allow them to wait inside. It must be admitted that the crowds had grown so great that the waiting room was terribly congested. In summer Brother André could receive them at the Oratory in his free time, but in winter it was closed. So they took to waiting for him in the tramway station on Queen Mary Road in front of the college. It was a strangely ornate little building with two steeple-like excrescences of tortured Victorian ironwork. What the transit company had spent on *décor* they saved on comfort. It was unheated and open on the side facing the tracks. Waiting there in sub-zero weather was a rigorous test of faith.

In 1907 a group of devout Montreal businessmen formed an association called "The Work of the Oratory" to assist Brother André in his plan to enlarge the building. This time Father Dion, who was rapidly succumbing to the simple faith of his porter, offered to take the petition to the Archbishop himself. As he left for his appointment, Brother André said, "Have you got a Saint Joseph's medal?"

"No," the Superior replied.

"Take this one," said the porter, "and hold it tightly in your hand while you are talking to His Excellency."

Archbishop Bruchési provisionally refused to sanction the work by saying that he must actually see the money raised. Thus he left the door open a crack. Brother André's faith and determination needed no more. By the spring of 1908 there was enough money to build a sort of wooden canopy back of the Oratory. Later in the summer this was enclosed in wooden walls sheathed with tar paper. In the autumn a small charcoal stove was set in one corner. Now the shrine could be used all winter.

The new nave was not an object of beauty. It was a hundred feet long and looked like an elongated cowshed attached to the rear of the original shrine. But the day of its dedication, November 22, 1908, was another of the great moments of Brother André's life. Yet, even while he happily listened as the Superior Provincial, Father Dion, said the blessing and celebrated Mass,

[83]

he pictured a basilica with a glorious dome second only to Saint Peter's in Rome.

The shrine continued to grow slowly but as inevitably as one of the great oaks in the mountainside. Electric light was installed, the walls of the nave were sheathed in sheet iron and Monsieur Joseph Paquette of Montreal presented a bronze bell weighing over a thousand pounds to summon the faithful.

In mid-July, 1909, Brother André was relieved of his duty as porter at Notre Dame and named official guardian of the Oratory. He left the porter's cell in which he had lived for thirty years and moved to a room in a small kiosk which had been built for the convenience of the pilgrims close to his beloved shrine.

But Brother André did not rest content. His next step was to request his Superior to assign a priest to offer daily Mass at the chapel. Father Dion threw up his hands. "I have none to spare," he said. "Every priest here is overworked."

"What about Father Clément?" asked the brother.

"You know he has gone blind," said Father Dion. "He cannot read his breviary or the Mass. He would be no use to you."

"Send him to me anyhow," said Brother André.

Father Adolphe Clément had been gradually losing his eyesight over a period of eight years, and had become almost blind. Though he was a strong middle-aged man, he was sadly reduced to being virtually a pensioner of Holy Cross unable to fulfill his priestly duties. The day after Brother André made his request, one of the brothers guided Father Clément up the steep road to the Oratory and brought him to Brother André. What followed is vouched for by the testimony of several eyewitnesses including Brother Philippe Saurette, a professor at Notre Dame at the time: "Brother André spoke to Father Clément, saying to him, 'I need you to help me with the sick and in my work at the Oratory.'

"Father Clément replied, 'What use can I be to you with my bad eyesight?' To which Brother André answered, 'Tonight

[84]

you will read your breviary and tomorrow you will say the Mass.'

"So it happened. Father Clément's eyes were cured and he was able to read his breviary that night and say the Mass the following day. . . . Father Clément became the right arm of Brother André in his work at the Oratory."

It is a matter of record that Father Clément was acting as Curé of the Oratory until 1926. That year he became Superior of Saint Joseph's Oratory and served in that position until 1934. For over twenty years he was able to read without eyeglasses, only needing them in the last years of his long life.

The Trial of Brother André

PAUL BRUCHÉSI

By the Grace of God and the Apostles, Archbishop of Mari-
anopolis
To M. the Canon J. T. Savaria
To the Rev. Father Joseph Lalande, S.J.
To M. l'Abbé Philippe Perrier.
For several years there has been a considerable movement of
pilgrims to the Oratory Saint-Joseph at Notre-Dame-des-Neiges.
Many people say they have obtained particular favors there. It
has also been reported to us that extraordinary cures have oc-
curred there.

Since it now seems opportune to us to proceed with a serious
examination of the facts, in order that we may enlighten the
piety of our faithful, we charge you to make a complete inquiry into everything which goes on at the Oratory Saint-
Joseph and also the extraordinary happenings which have occurred there.

We give you all the powers necessary to this end, especially
that of interrogating under oath all persons who you judge
will be able to inform you.

You will report to us on this inquiry and submit your conclusions.

THE reason for this directive was that by November 17, 1910,
the outcry against Brother André had reached a pitch which
forced the Archbishop to take action. The feeling against him,

irrational as it may appear, had been rising steadily for years. It seemed that the more people he cured, the more irritated those who disbelieved in him became. Within the community itself the ultra-conservative faction feared he might bring the college into disrepute. They were led by Brother Henri and Dr. Charette, who attacked Brother André openly. As Brother Philippe Saurette testified, "They did not refrain from mocking him openly about his 'treatment by greasing' because he recommended rubbing with Saint Joseph's oil. . . . Brother Henri had an impulsive temperament and made these scenes less from malice than from nervous tension. Dr. Charette was an excellent physician but very indiscreet. Brother André was well aware of these mockeries but paid no attention to them. As for me, I did not take the sorties of Brother Henri against Brother André seriously."

Others in the community and in the Church did worry however. As one prelate said, "There is danger of Brother André making Catholicism into a religion of massage." When the testimony of the Cause reached Rome you may be sure the head devil's advocate quoted that complaint.

So serious did the situation become that at one time there was talk of transferring the little brother to another community of Holy Cross, which would have broken his heart.

Meanwhile he kept on doing what his conscience told him was right. In this connection Arthur Saint-Pierre certified that on a later occasion a man was carried into Brother André's office in terrible condition. His back and legs were so distorted that he looked like a frog, and one side of his face was drawn into a hideous grimace by paralysis caused by nicotine poisoning. Saint-Pierre arrived in the anteroom just as the tall man walked out, made straight and strong in a moment of time. He was followed by a little group of people talking wildly, women crying. Saint-Pierre testified: "I saw Brother André in the midst of all this excitement. His face was overcome by emotion, tears streamed from his eyes. It was the only time I saw him so moved—he was habitually impassive.

"I took him aside and said jokingly, 'Brother André, you have made some more enemies.' Brother André replied, 'I could not do otherwise.' "

Then Brother André asked Saint-Pierre to find out the name of the man he had cured. The latter went over to the excited group, and came back to say, "His name is Laverdure" (The Greenery).

With the grin which always accompanied one of the terrible puns he loved to make, Brother André said, *"Il a reverdi."* (He has rebloomed.)

Soon the controversy about Brother André reached beyond the walls. Monsieur Azarius Claude testified: "Worldly people made very disagreeable remarks about Brother André, such as: 'Bah! Brother André is an ignoramus. He mixes himself up with the care of sick people and he is not a doctor.'

"When these remarks were repeated to Brother André, he said, 'They are quite right. I am ignorant. That is the reason the good God concerns himself with me. If there were anyone more ignorant, the good God would choose him in my place.' "

A large group of doctors—more Catholics than Protestants among them—made public complaint that the little brother was endangering the health of the people of Montreal. The discussion reached the newspapers, which charged Brother André with charlatanism and carried stories ridiculing him for the rubbing with Saint Joseph's oil and calling him "an old polisher." These stories finally succeeded in disturbing Brother André.

Then an even worse thing happened. In his great trouble Brother André confided in a lay friend, speaking of his own simple faith, the awe in which he held the power Saint Joseph used through him, and his convictions that these wonderful happenings were proof of the goodness of God, and the power of Saint Joseph. Poor Brother André had chosen his confidant badly. His supposed friend went about the city telling the story everywhere of the simple old fool who thought that Saint Joseph helped him to cure people with olive oil and a lead medal.

When Brother André heard of this it caused so deep a wound that years afterward the scar still remained. In tears he spoke to a sympathetic confrere: "My best friend, whom I trusted most of all, has betrayed me. His big mouth has spread to all the world the things which I said to him in confidence. You could not believe, you could not believe all the hurt that this has caused me."

Under this attack from within and without the community, Brother André was bewildered and bedeviled. Quite literally bedeviled, Father Bergeron believed, who saw in these calumnies a furious attack by Satan against Brother André's spiritual regeneration. At the same time he points out that such ordeals "only strengthened the virtues of humility, patience, obedience and the indomitable energy of the Servant of God."

Sister Leblanc testified that at the height of the storm a certain Monsieur Lacroix who for a long time had been troubled by severe pains in his head went to Brother André and begged him to touch his head and cure him. According to Sister Leblanc, "Brother André said, 'But haven't you seen in the newspapers all the stupidities reported against me and against my way of massaging? Don't ask me to touch you. Go to the chapel and pray to Saint Joseph and venerate the relic of Saint Joseph and you will be cured.'

"But M. Lacroix burst into tears; so disappointed was he that Brother André would not touch his head. Then Brother André felt a rush of pity for the invalid, and to console him took him by his shoulders and turned him toward the chapel. He gave him a little tap on the back of his head and said, 'Go along to the chapel and do what I told you to!'

"Well, according to the report of M. Lacroix, he felt better immediately and he was completely cured in the Oratory. He told me many times about this cure. . . . To my knowledge M. Lacroix is a man of integrity—a good Catholic and worthy of belief."

Such things only increased the hue and cry. Finally, when a group of doctors complained to the Board of Health, Archbishop Bruchési decided to act. In charging the commission he was careful to give them a free hand. In his directive there is no bias, either for or against Brother André.

The commission proceeded with great care and deliberation. They interviewed many witnesses to Brother André's wonderful cures and all the religious of Notre Dame, especially Father Dion. Though at first the Superior had doubted that his porter had a special mission, now he was stout indeed in his defense. Finally, the commissioners questioned and cross-questioned Brother André for several days. It must have been another *"grande épreuve"* for him, not only because of the doubts implied by the inquiry, but because it kept him from his appointed work and left the sick who had come for miles to see him standing outside his door.

One of the commissioners, hoping perhaps to save Brother André from sorrow and criticism, asked him gently, "Why do you not stop treating these people and leave them to God alone?"

Again, as so often before and afterward, Brother André answered, "I do what I feel I must."

He was also interrogated very particularly as to whether he felt the cures were his doing. At that the fire flashed from his eyes as he answered, "It is through Saint Joseph. I am nothing but his little dog."

To His Grandeur Monseigneur Paul Bruchési, Archbishop of Montreal:
   Monseigneur:
   Permit us to present the result of our inquiry relative to the happenings at the Oratory Saint-Joseph.

We are happy to be able to declare to Your Grandeur that everything we have found there appears to be well done to edify the piety of the faithful and develop their confidence in the puissant protection of Saint Joseph.

From what we have heard of the Reverend Father Dion, Provincial, as well as of the good Brother André, they seem to us to be animated by the highest spiritual ideals.

The most extraordinary happenings which we have studied seem indeed to be the result of a supernatural intervention due to the goodness and power of Saint Joseph. However, in these cases we cannot render an absolute judgment because the proofs are insufficient.

We think that a permanent bureau, where theological science and medical science are concentrated—since we dare to hope that Saint Joseph will continue to manifest the marvelous examples of his bounty—would be able to reach absolutely certain conclusions.

We attach the report of our inquiry, very humbly submitted to the judgment of Your Grandeur. . . .

The very humble servants in J. C.

> J. T. SAVARIA, CURÉ DE LACHINE
> ABBÉ PHILIPPE PERRIER
> J. LALANDE, S.J.
> 20 March, 1911.

Before giving his august judgment of the matter, the Archbishop studied the report with infinite care. Then he sent for Father Dion. Filled with anxiety the priest was shown into the great episcopal throne room where the Archbishop awaited him. Monseigneur Bruchési had one important question to ask: "If you order Brother André to stop these practices of his, will he obey you?"

"Yes," said Father Dion, unhappily. "He will obey."

The Archbishop then spoke with kindly wisdom which recalls King Solomon. "Then let him continue," he commanded, "for if this is the work of God it will flourish; if not, it will collapse of itself."

[92]

CHAPTER EIGHT

The Mustard Seed

Even before Brother André had been transferred from porter at the College to guardian of the Oratory, he often invited some of his lay friends to make an evening pilgrimage to the original little shrine with him. Carrying a lantern he led them up the difficult path to the Oratory where after praying to Saint Joseph they would follow the Stations of the Cross. At night in the chapel where the brightest light was the ruby lamp burning before Saint Joseph's statue this was an immensely moving experience. As the little brother progressed from one station to another saying the formal prayers and adding his own inspired petitions, he seemed to become transported so that he felt the sufferings of our Lord in his own body and soul, and communicated the sense of partaking in that terribly beautiful experience to the people who were with him. Sometimes they had a mystic feeling that the tiny, frail figure in black kneeling before the Stations was touched by a supernatural radiance.

Paul Corbeil, testifying before the Tribunal said, "One night I accompanied Brother André to his little chapel. [After our prayers] at the moment when he had closed the door I saw him standing in the attitude of one turning the key. For several seconds, as he stood there immobile in the obscurity of the night, he was illuminated by white rays of light such as we see

[95]

depicted in the paintings of the saints. That tableau created an extraordinarily unforgettable impression in me."

Some years later another friend of Brother André, Monsieur Adélard Fabre, had seen a similar phenomenon. He swore: "I was witness to a very extraordinary thing. . . . It was about half past nine in the evening. I saw Brother André kneeling on the floor of the nave of the Oratory at the foot of the Communion rail. He was enveloped by light. . . . I was standing about six feet from him. Brother André was in the light, I was not. There was no light in the Oratory except the lamp before the sanctuary. Far back, some votive candles were burning. The stream of light covering a distance of twenty feet stopped at Brother André. The statue of Saint Joseph was in obscurity, but the luminous rays seemed to be parted by the statue. I had a feeling that the statue was about to fall from the main altar toward Brother André. I went up to Brother André and touched his arm to warn him and lead him away.

"But Brother André did not speak or move. Terrified, I went to the sacristy in the hope of finding Brother Ludger, but he had gone to his room. As I left the sacristy to go and search for Brother Ludger I looked again through the door of the chapel. Brother André at that moment had moved to the altar of the Holy Virgin, next to the main altar. He was still enveloped in light.

"I found Brother Ludger who came with me to the Oratory. When we arrived there Brother André had left the altar of the Holy Virgin and was going to his room. At that moment the light disappeared.

"Brother Ludger and I discussed whether the light could have been rays of moonlight. But there was no moon that night."

In 1909 some of the friends of Brother André who had participated in his Holy Hour, founded the Confraternity of Saint Joseph at the Oratory, which was sanctioned by Archbishop

Alfred Bessette, 12, later Brother André, after his first Communion, about 1857.

The bakery, still unchanged, where Brother André worked as a boy.

The stone meeting house today at Saint-Grégoire-le-Grand, near Montreal, where Brother André was baptized in 1845.

Brother André after entering the novitiate of the religious of Holy Cross.

The first chapel, Saint Joseph's Shrine, on Mount Royal, 1912.

The old trolley station in the early 1900's.

Father Louage, Superior of Notre Dame College in Côte-des-Neiges, where Brother André served as porter for forty years.

Brother André at 63.

The chapel of Saint Joseph in 1914, Brother André at 69.

Brother André's room under the steeple in the garret of the chapel.

Ready for the road, 1921.

Bruchési on November 12 of that year. These devout men and women gave great impetus to the work of the Oratory.

Thus all through the troubled days of Brother André's ordeal by mockery and criticism the shrine continued to grow. The Fete of Saint Joseph was celebrated for the first time there on March 19, 1909. That evening a large group of worshipers carrying flaring torches climbed the mountain singing hymns in praise of the Patriarch.

Thereafter numerous great religious ceremonies were held at the Oratory. Each year more and more pilgrimages from increasingly distant places made their way up the mountain to venerate the Patriarch of Nazareth. And each year more gifts— beautiful religious statues and a relic said to be a piece of Saint Joseph's cloak—ornamented the chapel.

In October, 1910, the foundations for a monastery sixty by forty-five feet were dug. The completed building had a ground floor of cut stone; the two upper stories were brick. The building housed the growing staff of the Oratory.

The year 1912 was a great one for Saint Joseph and so for Brother André. In January was begun the publication of a little magazine, no more than a leaflet at first, describing the events of the Oratory. The first issue was only 300 copies, but within a year it had a circulation of 4,500. It has grown enormously with the passing decades. *The Annals of Saint Joseph* now has one of the largest monthly circulations in Canada—190,000 copies in the combined French and English editions.

That summer of 1912 a proper nave was built for the chapel, and it was dignified by a belfry with a graceful white steeple bearing a gleaming golden cross. Under the belfry, in a sort of attic, were quarters for Brother André.

Of all the rooms he ever occupied it seemed he loved that one best. It was a tiny cell, though it probably seemed quite luxurious to him. Its walls and ceiling were covered by the familiar embossed sheet iron. An open spiral stairway with no door led from it directly to the back of the nave. As Brother Saurette testified, "It was the ordinary room of a religious." Lighted by a naked electric bulb it contained two very narrow beds, a folding table covered with green baize which held two or three books. There were a pitcher for water and a wash basin with a drain pipe that ended in a pail which had to be taken downstairs to be emptied. There were also a plain wooden cupboard for clothes and medicines—Brother André's stomach was still capricious—and two hard wooden chairs.

Then came the brother's greatest luxury—a strangely ornate, two-burner oil stove. On it he cooked his meals which by now usually consisted of a little watered milk, and some lumps of flour dough boiled in plain water. A large crucifix hung on the wall near the stove, and on a small shelf close by stood Brother André's statue of Saint Joseph with a little lamp always burning before it. Facing the bed was a terribly realistic statuette of Christ during His Passion. Gazing at the tortured Figure in symbolic chains, covered with blood from His wounds, His face contorted with agony, Brother André would say again and again, "How the good Jesus suffered! How He suffered for us!"

The second bed, which could be shut off by a curtain, was frequently occupied by some sick man whom Brother André was trying to help. It was at this time that he began his great friendship with Joseph Pichette, who will now be recalled to the witness stand.

"The first time I heard of Brother André," Pichette testified, "a Madame Lucas came to my store and told me her arm had been cured by Brother André, who had advised her to put Saint Joseph's oil on it and drink a few drops, and to rub it with a medal of Saint Joseph. She advised me to go to see him. [I was very ill.] . . .

"I asked my wife to go to see Brother André and describe my malady. He told her that I must come myself. . . . I went on Sunday and told Brother André what I wanted. He asked me to wait until the other sick people had gone. Then he took me into his office and listened to my story. Then he told me to come back the next week if possible. I saw him many times that year. My health got no better. I was being treated by Dr. Georges Aubry. I suffered from the throat and the stomach. I coughed blood. The doctor told my sisters that my worst malady was my heart. He said I had the worst heart he had seen even in the hospitals in Paris where he had been. . . .

"Finally Doctor Aubry gave me to understand that I should prepare myself for the great voyage—there was nothing more he could do for me. I replied that I had one more person to see. . . . I told him it was Brother André. The doctor said to me, 'What do you think he can do? He is without instruction. I've heard them talk of him—they call him "the old fool." '

"I replied, that I had confidence that he could at least do more for me than the doctors. The doctor said, 'I warn you, look out, because in climbing to the Oratory you could drop dead in a moment.'

"The next Sunday afternoon I mounted to the Oratory . . . and told Brother André what the doctor had said. Then I added, 'If you will, I shall come here and not leave until I am cured or in my tomb. I can no longer live like this.'

"The brother replied, 'As you wish. If you want to come here you may sleep in my room at the chapel.'

"That is what I did. . . . He [Brother André] warned me not to walk and to eat carefully because there might be danger of my having a fatal accident. I could still digest nothing.

"During the nine days I spent at the Oratory there was no change. Brother André rubbed me with his hand two or three times a day. On the ninth day I think he rubbed me from eleven thirty in the evening until two thirty in the morning because I had told him things were not going so well.

"That night there were three of us in the room which was divided. I pulled a little mattress out of the cupboard and went to bed on the floor without a pillow.

"About four thirty in the morning Brother André was awakened by his alarm clock. He got up and we rose with him. That night he had brought in some fresh pork and veal with spices and seasonings and had boiled them in his pot. He peeled some potatoes and told me to put them in the broth at half past ten.

"At noon he came for dinner. He took a large plate, filled it with meat, potatoes and vegetables and gave it to me. In spite of my objections he told me to eat it, that all would go well. 'After you,' Brother André said, 'I shall eat.' And he ate three big pieces of bread.

"When we finished the repast Brother André told me I could walk. I felt fine and the afternoon passed without suffering. . . . Everything was marvelous.

"That evening he gave me the same nourishment and . . . I slept from ten thirty until his alarm clock woke me. I had not slept like that for nine days.

"The next day Brother André told me I could go. I went home on the streetcar almost to the other end of town. Then I took my bicycle and rode two miles to the Moreau Station. I took a train to the village of Saint Esprit. I had to get off five miles from my destination, and since there were no carriages I rode there on my bicycle. That was a long journey in the great heat of August.

"My wife wept, and I consoled her with the news that I was cured. In three weeks I gained eighteen pounds. The last three days of my vacation I went back to the Oratory as an act of grace for my cure. . . ."

On November 17, 1912, Archbishop Bruchési came to give his benediction to the new nave. It was at last a proper church lighted by windows with diamond panes of stained glass and room to seat two hundred people—many more were there that day standing crowded in the aisle and even on the steps outside. The tabernacle, too, had been greatly embellished. Above the main altar stood Saint Joseph holding little Jesus flanked by two angels. On his left the crowned Virgin in her blue robe spread her hands out in a gesture of pity and tenderness. On another small altar on the right was a statue of the Sacred Heart of Jesus as He had appeared to Saint Marguerite-Marie.

The venerable Archbishop in his splendid vestments was visibly torn by emotion as he performed the solemn rites. When he came to address the congregation his voice, trembling at first from age and sentiment, gained strength from his inspiration and rang out with the resonance of youth.

"I see here," the Archbishop said, "a movement of piety which heartens me. This Oratory could be justly compared to the mustard seed, so little in itself, which nevertheless produces a great tree.

"In the beginning a hand, pious and simple, placed a statue here. Each day people came to pray. Soon a little chapel rose on this spot. But the devotees of Saint Joseph became more and more numerous and it was necessary to enlarge the chapel many times. Today this is the last addition which I shall come to bless.

"But this work is only beginning, and I foresee in a future, perhaps not far distant, a church, a basilica worthy of Saint Joseph rising on Mount Royal and facing that most magnificent horizon.

"What shall I say of the miracles which take place here? If I deny them, these crutches and braces, witnesses of all the donors, will speak in my place. I had no need of the inquiry. It is certain that extraordinary things have taken place here, and even greater prodigies than physical cures . . . the greater things are the spiritual healings. Sinners have come here, and after prayer they have confessed and gone away purified. . . . I beg you to come here often to pray."

Brother André, as always on these great occasions standing in an obscure corner, must have been almost overcome, as Monseigneur Bruchési thus publicly declared his complete confidence in him, and for the first time sanctioned the little brother's fantastic dream of a basilica dedicated to Saint Joseph of Mount Royal.

Prevision

So many of the wonderful cures performed by Brother André have been mentioned here that they make it appear as if there were an uninterrupted series of these "miracles." This, of course, was not the case. Though throughout his long life many favors great and small were accorded him by the intercession of Saint Joseph, far more thousands of petitioners went away disappointed.

This was in accordance with the mystery of God's Will, whose reasons being beyond human comprehension must be accepted on faith. Miracles are not made to order, but are a unique sign of divine favor. Brother André fully realized this. Though, being a man of enormous goodwill, who would indubitably have liked to see every one of the sufferers who came to his mountain cured, he was content that any at all received these extraordinary favors, and often marveled aloud at the goodness of God.

However, Brother André almost always brought comfort to those he could not help physically by recalling to them the sufferings of our Lord. According to Father Cousineau's testimony, "Brother André often spoke with great emotion of the Passion of our Lord with tears in his eyes. I saw it myself, and heard of it from many pilgrims to the Oratory. From the beginning of the work at the Oratory Brother André recalled the Passion of our Lord to console the sick and lead them to submit to the Will of God. To those who suffered from pains in their heads he recalled that Christ had worn a crown of thorns; to those who suffered in their legs he said that Christ had been forced to carry His cross. Those who suffered the pains of heart disease were reminded that Christ's heart had been pierced by a lance."

The thing that upset Brother André most of all was when someone came to his office *demanding* to be cured as though he had the power to effect a miracle if he chose. Then his quick temper would blaze and his eyes flash. Arthur Ganz testified about one such occasion when he was present: "A lady came insisting that she be cured saying, 'I will not leave here before I am cured.'

"Brother André replied to her, 'Madame, you have been to consult one or two doctors; you have paid for your consultation, and you have not been cured. Here we charge nothing for a consultation. Does the good God owe you something?'

" 'Yes,' replied the lady. 'I go to Communion every morning.'

" 'Well then,' Brother André riposted, 'if the good God owes you something, go and collect it yourself. I am not in charge of collections for the good God.' "

Another instance of Brother André's choler at having the cures attributed to him was the time when one of the pilgrims said jokingly, "You are better than Saint Joseph. We pray to him and nothing happens, but when we come to see you we are cured."

Terrible was the rage of the little brother. His face turned scarlet and he rang his bell violently and banged the counter of his office. "Get out of here!" he fairly yelled. "It is Saint Joseph who cured you, not I. Get out! Throw him out!"

When the man had gone, Brother André was so shaken that Father Clément led him to his cell where he remained in bed for three unprecedented days.

In his testimony Father Cousineau gives an example of the

brother's humility before the clergy: "Father Clément told me the following: Father Frédéric de Ghyselde, a Franciscan from Trois-Rivières, paid a visit to Brother André at the Oratory. . . . Father Frédéric knelt before Brother André and asked his blessing. Brother André knelt also, saying, 'No, my Father, it is for you to bless me.' Father Clément surprised the two of them kneeling face to face."

In those cures which did take place there was no fixed pattern. Sometimes, as in the case of Joseph Pichette, the healing came after many days of prayer and much vigorous rubbing with Saint Joseph's oil. At other times a single application would be enough. Quite often Brother André did not even touch the sufferer, but merely looked at him and said, "You are well. Put down your crutches and walk!"

Still more extraordinary were the cures which were accomplished at a distance without his having even seen the sufferer. One such was described to this biographer by the former District Fire Chief, Léopold Lussier, a great friend and disciple of Brother André: "I went to his holy hour one evening, as I did almost every week," Lussier said. "On this occasion Brother André said to me, 'You look downhearted, Léo. Are you sick?'

" 'No,' I says, 'but I've got a six-month-old baby girl at home, and she is very sick. The doctor told me he cannot answer for her. Her temperature was 104 when I left. That is why I am here.'

"All Brother André answered was, 'Let us continue the holy hour.'

" 'Brother André,' I says, 'I want to go home and see how my baby is.'

" 'She will be all right,' he answered.

"So I stayed. When I got home—it was four and a half miles by streetcar—my wife said to me, 'Look at our daughter.'

"My little girl was sitting up in bed playing with her dolls and singing, full of joy. She had not a bit of fever.

" 'What time did this change occur?' I asked.

" 'At nine thirty this evening,' my wife answered.

"That was the hour at which I knelt beside Brother André in the chapel."

Joseph Moïse Robert testified that he once talked to Brother André about the cures. "I asked Brother André one day why certain sick people were cured so rapidly while others took a long time. Brother André replied, 'Those who are cured quickly often are people who have no faith or little faith, so their quick cures give them faith. On the other hand those who have solid faith are not cured so quickly, for the good God prefers to allow them to suffer so that they will be sanctified even more.' "

The idea of sanctification through suffering was always very close to Brother André's heart. Father Cousineau testified that on his deathbed the little brother said to him, "Yes, I suffer, but I thank the good God for according me the grace of suffering, for I have great need of it."

Brother André's favor of prevision has been mentioned before. It seemed that he always, or almost always, knew when a "miracle" would happen. Sometimes he was so sure that he would give the sufferer advice which would have been reckless had it not been inspired. Such was the case of a young workman from Saint Laurent who crushed his leg under a great stone. Gangrene set in and the doctors decided to amputate. The man consented in order to save his life.

According to the testimony of Brother Osée Coderre, "On his way to the hospital the sick man decided to stop at the Oratory and see Brother André. After hearing about the case, Brother André said, 'Go home and we will make a novena to Saint Joseph. There will always be time to cut off your leg.' The sick man returned to his home and at the end of the novena was completely cured. In gratitude this man and his two sons often came to work on the road of the Oratory."

Conversely, Brother André often had foreknowledge of death even to the exact hour. Nor did he withhold this knowledge

from the patient or his family. Instead he confided in them and
so comforted and inspired them by his faith that they accepted
the inevitable with resignation to the Will of God. Such was
the pathetic case of a child described in the testimony of Arthur
Ganz: "I accompanied Brother André to see a little girl eleven
years old who lived on Jeanne Mance Street. . . . Dr. Letendre
. . . was in attendance when we arrived. Brother André asked
the child what was wrong with her. She did not reply, and Dr.
Letendre said, 'The child has meningitis.'

"Brother André remarked, 'The child has no temperature
and does not suffer.'

"Dr. Letendre said, 'Brother André, I just took her temperature and I found that it had gone up to a higher degree than
a child can survive.'

"Brother André said, 'Doctor, I don't believe you.'

"The doctor then said, 'Brother André, permit me to take
the patient's temperature in front of you.' To the doctor's
amazement the child's temperature was completely normal.

"The child's mother spoke emotionally, 'Brother André, you
have saved my little girl.'

"Brother André replied, 'Madame, your child will die tomorrow morning between eight o'clock and half past eight, but she
will not suffer.'

" 'Brother André, save my child!' the mother cried.

" 'Madame, God alone knows the destiny of this child. Do
not oppose the wishes of the good God.'

"Well, the next day I went there and the child died at exactly
eight twenty-two in the morning, without any apparent suffering. . . . The mother was calm and resigned. When I told
Brother André that the little girl had died he replied simply,
'I know it.' "

On a later occasion Brother André visited a young man in
the hospital who was very ill with tuberculosis. After he had
prayed with him and rubbed him with Saint Joseph's oil, the
young man's temperature dropped to normal and his sufferings

ceased. Gladly and gratefully he thanked the brother, who said gently, "You are not cured. You will die a week from today, but do not be afraid. Saint Joseph is watching over you, and you will not suffer."

It happened just as Brother André had said. The youth died happily with full confidence in Saint Joseph.

Monsieur Michel Albert Trudel, who often accompanied Brother André on his trips and witnessed many such incidents as these, discussed this matter with the writer. Monsieur Trudel is a big, bald, long-nosed French Canadian, typical of the thrifty, conservative small shopkeeper. Yet he gave a beautifully mystic explanation of these prophetic utterances. M. Trudel said, "For myself, I believe that it was not that Brother André had a knowledge of the future, but that he was in constant contact with Saint Joseph who put the words on his lips."

Not all the people who came to the mountain were physically ill. Many had domestic problems; others had business difficulties and still more were troubled in their souls. These people poured out their hearts to Brother André who with his combination of supernatural faith and salty wisdom was able to help the great majority of them. To quarreling husbands and wives he often said, "A marital quarrel is like a room with a draft through it. It takes two doors to make a draft. If you close one of them it stops."

A woman brought her husband to see him complaining that he did not go to Mass often enough.

"How often do you receive Communion?" Brother André asked him.

"Once a year at Easter," he replied sullenly. "The Church says that is sufficient."

"If you only ate once a year you'd be very sick," Brother André observed. "You are starving your soul."

He was as ready to pray to Saint Joseph for those in financial straits as for sick people; for he realized that extreme poverty can be as great a hardship as physical suffering. Nor did it seem that Saint Joseph was always indifferent to such pleas. One of those who believed that Saint Joseph helped him is the author, Arthur Saint-Pierre, who now owns a pleasant house in Montreal. In his case the favor came with stunning directness. Saint-Pierre says, "I left school at thirteen and became in turn a farmer, streetcar conductor and journalist. For several years I was with *La Presse* as their Ottawa correspondent. Then I lost my job. I was desperate and went to the Oratory to pray for help. Father Laurin saw me and said I came providentially. His Superior had charged him with writing a history of Saint Joseph's Oratory, and he was having great difficulty. 'My work keeps me distracted,' he said. 'Will you write it?'

"From that time on I never lost an hour of work, hard times and good. I consider it a special favor."

When asked: *Do you desire the beatification of the Servant of God?* Saint-Pierre stoutly declared: "I must say that I appeal for the intercession of Brother André each time I pray at Saint Joseph's Oratory. . . . I never fail to pray at Brother André's tomb. Of course, like all the world I await the judgment of Rome on Brother André, but because of what I know of the favors obtained at the Oratory, I am convinced that certain [of those favors] are due not only to the intercession of Saint Joseph but also to the influence of Brother André.

"I must say that I desire the beatification of Brother André because I believe it would render justice to his extraordinary virtues, and to his life completely devoted to love for his neighbor."

Other pecuniary favors saved families from bankruptcy, and at least one man, a Jew, from suicide. M. Trudel, sitting in the modern chrome and steel appliance store in which he is a partner, said that in 1942, after Brother André's death, the business had great difficulty getting any appliances to sell because of wartime shortages. His senior partner, Monsieur Joseph Robert, said, "We will put our dear friend Brother André on the payroll. Perhaps he will help us."

[109]

"Very soon," M. Trudel continued, "we had more goods than we could sell. What to do?"

"M. Robert solved it. 'We will raise Brother André's salary and make him a salesman.'

"Ever since then our business has prospered. Brother André is still on the payroll. Someone from the Oratory comes once a month to collect his salary."

According to Archbishop Bruchési, Brother André's greatest work was in bringing sinners back to the Church and spreading the cult of Saint Joseph. Father Elphège Labonté told of the wisdom with which Brother André gently led these errant souls back to God. "He said to me," Father Labonté testified, 'Do not demand of a man why he does not go to Mass more often. Simply ask him, "When did you last take Communion?" In this way you will get him talking and win his confidence.' I have used his method ever since."

When his confreres protested that Brother André prayed so long that his health was endangered, he replied, "Oh if you knew how many sinners there are to pray for and how desperate is the need."

Yet he was not grim even about this serious matter. Arthur Saint-Pierre tells of how with laughter in his eyes Brother André said, "When one prays for sinners one does not pray for strangers."

When Father Cousineau became Superior of the Oratory, Brother André told him of the manner in which he reasoned with these troubled souls. "He said to me," Father Cousineau testified, " 'When I see that I have business with a sinner, I remind him that his soul was redeemed by the Blood of our Lord. What would you say if someone gave you a beautiful house and embellished it with precious furnishings, and then you, you let in a herd of hogs? Well then, that's exactly what you have done. In your soul, which is the house of the good God, the demons have become the masters.

" 'Then I urge them to confess themselves and receive Communion. Very often I end by telling them of the Passion of our Lord.'

"Then the good brother with tears in his eyes related the Passion to me in a hushed voice. After that he asked me if he should continue thus. I answered in the affirmative."

Then Father Cousineau told of the time when Brother André went to visit Monsieur Joseph Dieudonné Hébert of Granby, Quebec. He arrived at the Hébert house at five thirty in the morning and immediately proposed going to early Mass. Reluctantly M. Hébert agreed to take him to the church. On the way Brother André suggested that they receive Communion together. His host answered that he received Communion quite often when he was especially favored by fortune. Brother André said, "Suppose a blind man who was very rich offered you a hundred thousand dollars for your eyes. Would you take it?"

"No," said M. Hébert.

"Would you even take a hundred thousand for an arm or a leg?"

"No."

"Or your hearing, or your speech, or any of your senses?"

"No."

"Then if we add them all up these things which the good God has given you are worth about a million dollars. Is that not enough?"

Monsieur Hébert was deeply moved. But he still held back. "I cannot receive Communion without making confession. I cannot do that because I know my curé is not at the church. He is away on vacation."

"I know he is there," said Brother André.

When they reached the church they found that the curé had returned unexpectedly. "Knowing himself vanquished M. Hébert confessed and received Communion."

After Mass he proudly presented Brother André to his curé. The priest received the little brother rather coldly, which made Monsieur Hébert boiling mad. At home again he spoke angrily about the priest's manners. Brother André said, "The priest is the representative of Jesus Christ; it is not right to criticize him."

However, Monsieur Hébert was so furious that he made another derogatory remark. Very seriously Brother André spoke, "M. Hébert, I love you very much and I am happy to visit your home, but if you criticize the priest again I will never return to your house."

M. Pichette told the court of a phrase in which Brother André summed up his gentle philosophy of salvation: "Someone said to him, 'Is it necessary to be so holy to go to heaven?' To which Brother André replied, 'When a person does his best, he can have confidence in the good God. What hurts Him most is to think that we will not go to heaven because we have not done our best.'"

The Travels of Brother André

Did the Servant of God frequently leave the Community?

This was a key question because it touched on both the matter of Brother André's heroic obedience and his heroic temperance as a good religious. In Rome as well as Montreal the devil's advocate argued that the little brother "lived on the fringe of community life," because he was absent a great deal and he enjoyed his trips too much. Witness after witness answered, "Yes, he was often away. But never without the permission of his Superior and never for his own enjoyment, but always to bring help to those who suffered or to spread the cult of Saint Joseph."

Very early in his religious life, long before the first little shrine was built on Mount Royal, Brother André began his practice of calling on those who were too ill to come to him. When he went on errands for the College of Notre Dame he would often stop at one or two houses where he had been asked to cure or at least comfort a very sick person.

As his fame spread, these requests became more frequent; and after his long day receiving the pilgrims in his little office at the Oratory, he would scurry around the city, stopping at the great hospitals, the little humble houses of the poor, or the fine mansions of the rich to do his best. Until he was seventy years old he made the journeys by streetcar or on foot.

From about 1915 on, a group of Brother André's devoted friends made themselves into a car pool for him. Every evening, except Friday, which was devoted to his Holy Hour and the Way of the Cross, one of them would call for him when his "office hours" ended, and chauffeur him about the city. After many calls at hospitals or stricken homes, the little brother would usually visit the house of his driver. Deliberately throwing off the weight of misery which the sufferers had laid upon his shoulders the spry old man would behave with boyish gaiety, cracking those outrageous puns of his, or wandering in the small suburban gardens touching the flowers reverently and saying, "How beautiful! How good the good God is!"

When they returned to the Oratory, after a day which was always seventeen hours long, Brother André would invite his friend in for prayer and meditation. He would light a candle, saying, "This is designed to burn for just an hour," and stick it on a pew. Then he would kneel before the Blessed Sacrament, and remain in motionless ecstasy until the candle gutted out.

Though Brother André had passed the Biblical toll of years before he began making his rounds in the automobiles of his friends, he did it less for comfort than for the sake of speed. Speed he loved, as Pope Pius XII did, and for the same reason, that it gave him more time for the work of God. Fire Chief Raoul Gauthier occasionally took him on an errand of mercy in his official vehicle. The little brother was as delighted as a boy dashing along in the bright red car with the traffic parting before them at the clang of its gleaming bell.

Monsieur Trudel, who sometimes drove him on longer trips through Canada and the United States, says, "When we were going somewhere I was always careful to have the car full of gas so we need not stop. He did not even want to stop for meals, so I kept coffee in a thermos in the back seat. We would have that and biscuits for lunch on the wing. Mostly he sat beside me saying his Rosary while we hurtled over the twisting roads. You had to drive at ninety to satisfy him."

Brother André knew all the policemen and they knew him, knew that he was hurrying for a good purpose; so he was never arrested, except once. That time he said laughing to M. Trudel, "I was arrested yesterday."

"You!" Trudel exclaimed in surprise.

"Yes, me. The policeman wanted my autograph."

Arthur Ganz says that once when they crossed the Victoria Toll Bridge he did not have the right coin. Brother André said, "I have it," and paid the collector. About halfway across the bridge he suddenly said, "I forgot my change."

"We can't turn back in this traffic," groaned Ganz.

Brother André laughed: "I gave him a medal of Saint Joseph."

Ganz, who speaks both French and English colloquially, though with the thick accent of his native Switzerland, was one of Brother André's most frequent companions. In an emergency the brother might call him in the middle of the night to convey him to some stricken home, and Ganz would respond like an old fire horse. One time Brother André clapped him on the shoulder with deep affection and said, "It is not only the Pope who has a Swiss guard, I have one, too."

Another favorite of the brother was Léopold Lussier, a district fire chief like his father before him. Lussier, who is over six feet tall with the build of a football player, says that when Brother André was approaching ninety the doctors forbade him to climb stairs because of a heart condition. After that when they came to a house where the invalid was in bed on the second or third floor, Lussier would effortlessly sling the tiny, ninety-five pound religious over his shoulder and carry him up the stairs. "When we got back to the Oratory," Lussier said, "Brother André would say jokingly, 'I'll race you up the mountain.'

"When Brother André was sick I used to rub him with Saint

Joseph's oil. Father Labonté might call me and say, 'Brother André wants to see you.'

"I'd go to his little room which was heated by a radiator and an electric heater, take my coat and collar off and rub him until the sweat was dripping off my nose. He would say, 'Don't be afraid, rub harder!' And then, 'Oh you're tired, are you?'

"I'd say, 'I'm not tired. I'm numb.'

"Brother André seemed to be able to rub people all day, though he looked so small and weak."

Lussier described one of the most unhappy services Brother André ever performed. The steamer *Cymbeline* caught fire at Vicker's Dry Dock in Montreal. It was a considerable blaze imperiling other ships and docks, and the waterfront itself. Fire Chief Gauthier was standing on her deck directing his men who were playing thick hoses down the open hatches when *Cymbeline* disintegrated in a tremendous explosion that hurled the fire chief and three of his men skyward in a fiery fountain of blazing timbers and red-hot chunks of steel, their tumbling bodies black against the incandescent sparks which fell hissing into the river.

When the fire was finally brought under control, the firemen dragged the river for the bodies of their comrades and their chief. Three corpses were recovered, but that of Chief Gauthier was lost. Meanwhile someone had gone for Brother André, who stood on the edge of the dock with his black soutane whipping in the wind sadly watching their efforts. One of the district chiefs said to him, "I'm afraid we'll never find him. His body must have been carried downstream by the current."

Tight-lipped Brother André replied, "I don't think so."

Then he said a prayer and threw a Saint Joseph's medal as far as he could into the swiftly moving water. Pointing to the spot he said, "He will come up there."

Let Lussier tell the rest: "I was there, all of us were, out in boats. We had dragged that spot twenty times. Yet the following morning the body of our chief appeared floating on the water."

Soon after he became official guardian of the Oratory, Brother André began the series of visits to the United States which became his annual custom and spread the cult of Saint Joseph widely in that country, bringing thousands and later tens of thousands and now millions of American pilgrims to the shrine.

The first time he went the thought was that he must have a rest from his eighteen-hour-a-day labors and the thousands of sick and unhappy people who besieged his little office. He got precious little rest.

He went to stay with his sister in Woonsocket, near Providence, Rhode Island. His fame had preceded him. The Rhode Island newspapers got wind of his presence there and soon the house was besieged by sufferers. Brother André said, "Line them up and I will see them all."

As the Americans filed past, he gave them his customary advice to rub themselves with the medal and the oil. It is reported that he received two hundred people a day during his "vacation." In addition he visited the local hospitals and those in Providence.

It soon became apparent that Saint Joseph was as close to him in the mill towns of Rhode Island as he had been on Mount Royal. In testimony taken before the subsidiary tribunal in Providence, Eusèbe Viau swore: "I know, among others, of the cure of Agnes Leblanc, my adopted daughter whom we brought up. This young girl began going blind and deaf at the age of eighteen because of uncontrollable eczema. She was condemned [to blindness] by Dr. Boucher of Woonsocket and the specialists of the Rhode Island General Hospital, where she remained under observation for three weeks. They returned her to us as incurable. This happened about 1916.

"It was at my home that Brother André saw her about a year later. The young girl was still blind. Brother André assured us that she would see again clearly. Her vision returned about a year later. Little by little she began to see more clearly to the point where she could easily read and write. She had not been given any further medical treatment during that time. She still sees clearly today [thirty years later] and attributes her cure to Brother André, who in turn attributes it to Saint Joseph.

"I do not know how he could produce these prodigies. When one saw Brother André pray, almost always on his knees, his face was transfigured, almost angelic. I believe that his life was an uninterrupted penitence."

Before the same tribunal Lionel Maynard testified that he was stricken by the rot [tuberculosis] of three spinal vertebrae as diagnosed by two eminent Rhode Island specialists. He spent four weeks in the hospital with no benefit and left on crutches.

He stated: "The Metropolitan Life and Prudential Life Insurance companies both pronounced me an incurable invalid. Then Monsieur Philippe Brouillard persuaded me to go to see Brother André, who was staying with M. Boulet at Arctic. On my entering the room where the sick people were gathered Brother André came straight to me. He asked what was wrong, and then told me to get up. At his demand I stood with the assistance of my crutches. Then Brother André told me to give him the crutches, and made me walk without support, faster and faster, until I was almost running. I was without support and without pain, in full view of a hundred people who burst into tears.

"That same evening, less than an hour later, I recited my Rosary on my knees without support before my marveling family. I gave my crutches and corset brace to Brother André, who took them back to the Oratory."

This testimony recalls the statement of M. Trudel that, "Sometimes we came back from those trips with a carload of crutches."

An even more remarkable cure was that of William Lord of Chicopee, Massachusetts. He had been in bed four years lying in a partial coma without memory and speech. After a visit from

Brother André Mr. Lord woke up the next morning singing a French song. He thought he had been asleep only one night.

These are but three isolated instances of hundreds of cures which are attributed to Brother André in the United States. From New England to California, where he went in 1921, the eyewitness stories are the same. As the newspapers reported these things, great crowds gathered wherever he went. On one visit to Jersey City, the whole town turned out with decorations and flags flying in his honor. When he returned from that trip he confided in Father Clément with charming naïveté, "You know I had great luck. Jersey City was *en fête* in honor of somebody or other. It was very gay."

However, as the public tributes increased so did the pressures on Brother André. He hardly had a moment's peace with his family or, what from his point of view was infinitely worse, time for his private devotions. Mr. Maynard testified that, "When he was staying with me, all the time he was not seeing the sick, he was in his room at prayer."

No matter where he was Brother André always insisted on being taken to early Mass at six in the morning, and he frequently attended evening devotions as well. Father Frank Cornish of Keeseville, New York, described how the first time Brother André came there he asked as they walked toward the presbytery, "What time will you have devotions in the church tonight?"

"What devotions?" asked the priest.

"Don't you have devotions at all tonight?" asked the surprised religious.

"This is a weekday, Brother," Father Cornish reminded him.

Brother André pointed to the houses of the village climbing the hillside in the early evening dusk. "Look," he said, "every house is lighted. Should not God's house be lighted, too? People are going and coming between their homes; don't you think they would come to visit God?"

"We have a Holy Hour one Thursday every month," said the priest defensively.

"That is fine, but I think God would like one every week better."

Father Cornish argued that it was useless. "We have a hard enough time getting them to church Sundays," he said.

That mulish look came on Brother André's face. He stopped dead in his tracks and said, "I won't move until you promise me to have a Holy Hour *every* week."

Father Cornish was in a most embarrassing position. He could not possibly leave as revered a religious as the famous little brother standing in the middle of a street in his own parish. It was sheer blackmail! Weakly he made the promise.

The result astounded him. Brother André attended the first Holy Hour and a big crowd turned out. Father Cornish put that down to the brother's presence. But people kept coming every week after Brother André had gone home. They even drove over from neighboring villages.

When Brother André came back to Keeseville again, Father Cornish told him how right he had been. "How did you know it would work?" he asked.

Brother André permitted himself an enigmatic smile.

For these trips Brother André had no suitable clothes of his own. He used to borrow a heavy, oversized black overcoat and a square derby hat from a friend. In this outfit he would dash around in his lively, youthful way looking like a little boy dressed in his father's clothes until you saw his face wrinkled by age and the sufferings he had accepted for others.

On the longer trips he often went by train, always accompanied by one of his devoted friends. M. Laporte described his first overnight journey with Brother André. After a light supper in the dining car they retired to their compartment, where they knelt side by side at the berth for their evening prayers.

After a long time Laporte became exhausted and timidly asked, "Don't you think we have prayed long enough?"

"You must be very tired," Brother André said gently. "Go to bed now and turn out the light. I will be a few moments more."

Laporte climbed into the upper berth and fell sound asleep. Once he half waked in the night and in the flash of station lights saw his small companion still kneeling beside the swaying berth.

When Laporte awoke in the morning, Brother André was already up. Face covered with lather he was shaving with a straight razor. Horrified, Laporte sat up and said, "Stop it! You'll cut your throat with that thing."

Balancing easily in the jolting train and looking boyishly pleased with himself, Brother André said, "I can shave any-where. And without a mirror, too!"

People gave Brother André a great deal of money for his Oratory on these trips. According to Arthur Ganz he never counted it. "Five cents or five hundred dollars was the same to him. He'd stuff it in his little black satchel. When I was with him he always made me take charge of it, because he thought it infringed his vow of poverty to have money on his person."

As Brother André advanced in years, the crowds that came to see him grew ever greater. They followed him in the streets begging for his autograph, and even tried to snip off bits of his clothing. This made his temper blaze. "It's ridiculous," he said. "You would suppose I was something special. What can they want with an old piece of cloth?"

Once at least the pressure became too great for him. He was staying with his cousin Henri J. Bessette in Holyoke, Massachusetts. All day for several days people had been standing outside the house waiting to crush through the little parlor and touch his hand. That evening he had promised to attend a reception for a thousand people at the Nanotuck Hotel.

Late in the afternoon he was so overcome by weariness that his alarmed cousin sent for a physician. "You must on no account go out tonight," the doctor said. "I will not answer for you, if you do."

"I cannot disappoint so many people," Brother André replied. "I am going."

In the tightly jammed ballroom of the hotel, Brother André felt even worse. When the time came for him to speak, he got to his feet, but immediately sank down in a chair. He rested for a moment or two, then summoning all his force rose again and began to talk to the crowd in his simple, pious way.

But even the holiest men have human limits. Suddenly his voice died out and he quietly collapsed. The horrified crowd stood staring at a little heap of old black clothing crumpled on the ballroom floor.

Happily the brother had only fainted. Two days secreted in a hospital, while crowds stood outside his cousin's house, restored him. He was able to go on about his Master's business.

The Mountain Moves

I<small>N</small> May, 1915, most of the world was at war. Along five hundred miles or more of trenches, from the English Channel to the Swiss border and from the Baltic Sea to the Danube, the crash of high explosives continually shocked the air. In that same May the boom and rumble of dynamite shattered the quiet of Mount Royal and a great piece of rock was split off the face of the cliff. The sound was similar to the crashing guns, but the object was as different as destruction from creation or death from everlasting life.

The explosion on Mount Royal was, in fact, the concrete beginning of Brother André's dream of a temple worthy of Saint Joseph. As far back as 1912 the dream had begun to take shape on the drawing boards of the architects, D. Viau and J. Venne. Their conception was magnificent enough to suit even Brother André's ambition for Saint Joseph. It envisioned a great Renaissance church, set in the flank of the mountain, whose dome would top the crest itself showing a lighted cross to the city which lay beyond. But, with the shrewd practicality that the French admire as the virtue of prudence, it was so designed as to be accomplished not all at once, but step by step.

Because this was a work of faith, and his faith first of all, Brother André was a member of the Council of the Oratory. Nor did he try to push them too far too fast, for he had absolute confidence that the work would be completed in Saint Joseph's own good time. However, even to begin such a project in the midst of a great war in which Canada was fighting beside England for her very life and freedom showed a daring that would have been foolhardy had it not been assured by sublime faith. For the structure was expected to cost three million dollars—it has, in fact, cost ten million to date—and by the orders of Archbishop Bruchési it must not become a charge on the diocese but must be financed by the contributions of the faithful given freely with no pressure drives.

The first step was to build the Crypt Chapel, in itself a large church 200 feet long, 118 feet wide and 40 feet in height, capable of accommodating two thousand people. Before the work began Brother André's little chapel was hauled on greased timbers to one side. The contractor was Monsieur Ulric Boileau. His men began blasting a foundation out of the mountain on which the crypt would stand. In May, 1916, Archbishop Bruchési blessed the cornerstone of the chapel. It was to be built of cut stone and designed in the Renaissance style. The façade, which was to be approached by an imposing flight of wooden steps, would have great arched windows and be flanked by round bastions on either side.

During the course of the work Brother André spent every moment he could spare overseeing the construction. He did not even wait to have five-thirty breakfast with the community, but stuffing a few biscuits in his pocket, would go down to the crypt before the first workmen arrived. He also spent the two-hour break in his office hours from noon to two o'clock at the job, eating no regular meal during the entire day.

Often at night after the workmen and the pilgrims, too, had gone home, the little brother would wander over the gaping, unfinished floor, looking at the scaffolding and timbers, the piles of stones and cement and the huge machines by the light of an oil lantern carried by one of his friends. As a result of his nocturnal prowling he had a singular mishap one evening. It was brought before the Tribunal by a question asked by the devil's advocate of M. Pichette:

Promoter of the faith: *Had the Servant of God already seen apparitions of the demon or been vexed by him?*

Monsieur Pichette: "When they were enlarging the presbytery [in 1928], we went, Brother André and I, to pray in the Crypt. In returning [to the presbytery under alteration] we passed a place where they had removed the old flooring leaving a gap about fifteen feet by ten feet wide and three deep. Along its edge was a piece of plank about a foot and a half wide. We stood on it with our backs against the wall while Brother André explained to me how the old and the new construction would be joined together. He added, 'How the good God is good!'

"He had not time to finish the phrase, when he left me suddenly as though he wanted to fly over the gaping pit in front of us. He left me without any movement of jumping at all. Brother André landed on the opposite side striking his head against the planking and remained there with his legs hanging down, while I ran around to his assistance.

"Brother André had a bruise on his forehead and his legs were also hurt. He passed his hand over his forehead and the bruise disappeared.

"For my part, this leap appeared to me to be a dozen feet, and I could not understand how a man could jump twelve feet. I remained convinced that Brother André had attempted a jump that was, to say the least, imprudent, and I said no more about it.

"The following year when I was at the Oratory, Brother André lent me the key to his room. While there I looked at several of his books. He showed me one book, the life of Sister Marie-Marthe Chambon, which he handed to me with one page specially marked. I took the book and at the indicated page I read that the devil had also transported this sister and made her suffer. So, at last, I understood that the leap Brother André had made the year before must have been caused by the demon."

[129]

The chapel was completed in good time. In April, 1916, the newly formed Corporation of the Oratory, owned by Holy Cross, had purchased 500,000 square feet of land on the mountain from the College of Notre Dame for $210,000. The actual construction began in January of that year. In December, 1917, a magnificent statue of Saint Joseph, nine feet high in white Carrara marble, arrived from Italy. It was executed as an act of grace by the Italian sculptor M. Giacomini and presented by a Sulpician priest, M. Félicien Laliberté. There had been great anxiety as to its safety, for German U-boats were sinking a hundred thousand tons of Allied shipping a month. As the official history of Holy Cross states, "It arrived December 5, 1917 . . . Saint Joseph took the matter in hand without any doubt."

Incidentally, in the year 1917 the Oratory received 21,624 letters from the faithful, of which 2,631 gave thanks for cures or favors obtained through the intercession of Saint Joseph.

On December 16, 1917, Archbishop Bruchési blessed the chapel and the statue. It was very different from the little church he had sanctified only five years before. Built as a bastion at the foot of the great temple of the future, it was called the "Crypt" because of its position and massive architecture. From its low vaulted ceiling splendid chandeliers illuminated its cavernous interior. Above the rich main altar in a blaze of light stood the heroic statue of Saint Joseph holding the Christ Child, its pure white marble backed by a great aureole of gleaming, golden rays. Far more than the two thousand people for which it was designed crowded the Crypt that day and knelt beyond its open doors.

The man whose faith had built it sat inconspicuously in the last choir stall on the Epistle side. For the next twenty years, Brother André chose that humble place for his nightly prayers.

With the irony which often saddens the hearts of men the first important ceremony in the new Crypt was the funeral of

Father Dion. The death of his good Superior who, doubting him at first, had become his strongest advocate and the staunch supporter of the Work of the Oratory, was a great blow to Brother André.

Father Dion was succeeded as Provincial of Holy Cross and Superior of the Oratory by Father Alfred Roy, a man with gentle eyes beneath a fine broad forehead. There always seemed to be a smile lurking at the corners of his lips. He was a fervent disciple of Saint Joseph, and, like Father Dion, he understood Brother André and fully co-operated with him in diffusing devotion to the holy Patriarch.

Under him the Oratory continued to expand. To quote the official history:

> By now the work of the Oratory was forever assured. One already felt the hope that soon the walls of a basilica would crown the sanctuary dedicated to Saint Joseph by the piety and generosity of the faithful. It was the spontaneous gifts of the Canadians which had made the work possible without loans or any special appeal to the generosity of the public. Since the money had been raised, not by princely gifts, but by the accumulation of the little alms of the people, why not trust to them for the future? This was always the policy of Brother André, of Father Dion and of their successors.

It appeared that the Crypt would meet the needs of the Oratory for the next few years; so without forgetting the great design of the basilica, which Brother André predicted he would see before he died, Father Roy set to work embellishing the approaches and acquiring more land. The ground around the Crypt was terraced and planted in lawns and flowers. A high wrought-iron fence with wide gates swinging from granite pillars was erected along Queen Mary Road, and two little stone stations were built to shelter the pilgrims waiting for streetcars. In 1922, a huge bronze statue of Saint Joseph by the sculptor Alfred Laliberté was placed on a pedestal of white granite dominating the long carpet of turf and the tree-shaded roads which swept up to the terraced base of the Crypt.

Morgan Powell in the Montreal *Star* described the Fete of Saint Joseph held at the Crypt in March, 1921. At six o'clock in the morning he observed "an interminable line" of pilgrims making their way up the mountain through the morning mists.

> . . . From time to time they halted to get their breath and then moved forward in their arduous march up the steep hill to the sanctuary.
>
> To the right of the Oratory, at the top of a steep wooden stairway stood a man dressed in black. His slight figure was enveloped from shoulders to feet in a somber overcoat. With arms crossed he raised his face to the splendor of the sunrise. . . . Then his eyes perceived the long, sinuous line of pilgrims advancing slowly toward the heights. The arms of the mysterious spectator were raised slowly toward God in a gesture of adoration. . . .

After the ceremonies Morgan Powell interviewed Brother André in his office. One of his first questions concerned Brother André's age, which was seventy-five.

"Old?" said the little brother. "I am not old. Look you! Seven and five that makes twelve, which is to say I am twelve years old. . . . Tired? Is one ever tired in the service of the Master? Oh yes, I am up before the dawn. . . . You ask if I cure people. You must not talk like that. Just say I hope that they go away happy. . . ."

In the springtime of 1922, the freshet of small gifts had accumulated into a lake of capital large enough to justify beginning work on the basilica. Once again the muffled boom of dynamite sent bits of the mountain flying skyward as the engineers began excavating thousands of tons of solid rock for the huge foundation. The occasional explosions were supplemented by the continuous racket of pneumatic drills, stone crushers, steam shovels, and the roar of loose rocks precipitated down wooden chutes to the waiting trucks. These labors continued for almost three years.

On August 31, 1924, the three hundredth anniversary of the naming of Saint Joseph as the patron saint of Canada was celebrated at the Oratory. Thirty-five thousand people, the greatest number who had ever climbed the mountain until then, knelt while Monseigneur Pietro di Maria, the Apostolic Delegate to Canada, blessed the cornerstone of the basilica.

After the ceremony the brilliantly robed prelates and the silk-hatted representatives of the Canadian Government had their photograph taken on the steps of the presbytery. Off at one edge of the picture, almost lost in the crowd, wearing his old black soutane with his white hair making an aureole in the brilliant sunshine stands Brother André.

However, when the first stone of the walls was set in place, Brother André himself wielded the trowel while the architects Viau and Venne and the religious of Holy Cross looked on. The little brother, wearing his oversize black overcoat and square black hat, spread the mortar and, smiling broadly, looked up to say, "I never was much of a mason."

The Holy Hour on Friday evening, so dear to Brother André's heart, was officially inaugurated in October, 1923, by Archbishop Georges Gauthier of Montreal. To quote the Chronicles of the Oratory:

> The initiative for this beautiful act dates back a long time. Dear Brother André made it his custom to go to the Chapel on Friday evening to spend an hour before Jesus—Host. One night he invited two friends to accompany him in these pious exercises. These were the pioneers who promised to return the following week. . . . Their number gradually increased, largely due to the efforts of the corps of firemen who are so devoted to Saint Joseph. . . . More than 150 persons were present. . . .

In 1925, there is the following entry:

More than 800 persons assisted at the Hour of Adoration which was held from eight to nine in the evening. Brother André presided over the exercises of the Way of the Cross followed by a great crowd making atonement. . . .

Indeed from the time the Crypt was finished the influence of the Oratory multiplied in geometric progression. In 1926 more than a million pilgrims visited it, and the number of Communions given was 119,000.

Did the Servant of God manifest undue pride at the success of the Oratory?

Father Cousineau: "To my knowledge Brother André never took vainglory from the success of the Work of the Oratory. . . . I never heard him speak of the Oratory as 'my work' or 'my operation.' Never to my knowledge did Brother André calculate the alms or moneys given to the Oratory. I remember that after one ceremony at the Oratory His Excellency Monseigneur Gauthier, Archbishop of Montreal, remarked to a group of guests of whom I was one, 'If ever I am called as witness in the Cause of Beatification of Brother André, I would be able to say that he never posed as a personage.' "

Witness after witness also testified that Brother André took no credit for the beautiful temple which his faith had built upon Mount Royal. He always said, "It is the work of Saint Joseph."

However he showed a boyish loyalty to the Oratory. Arthur Ganz was with him one evening in the Crypt. Brother André stood meditating before the wall full of braces and crutches donated by people who had been cured. "Is it not wonderful?" he said. "How good the good God is!"

To tease him Ganz remarked, "They have a lot more at Sainte-Anne-de-Beaupré."

Brother André flashed back, "Think of how much longer they have been there!"

Temptation

WHEN the old chapel was relocated in 1915, Brother André moved from his room above it to a cell in the presbytery. From this time forward he formed the pattern of life which he maintained until two weeks before his death. It was rigorous for a man of seventy, which was his age in 1915. For a man over ninety years old it was incredibly arduous. The details of his day appear in Father Cousineau's answer to the question, *What works of mercy did the Servant of God perform?*

Father Cousineau: "I can say in a general way that Brother André's . . . works of mercy were more spiritual than corporal . . . with the sick Brother André applied himself to counsel them, to console them and to heal them throughout forty years. The principal work of corporal charity practiced by Brother André was the reception of the sick at his office in the Oratory and the visits to the sufferers in their homes which he made almost every day. So you will better understand the work of Brother André at the Oratory, I will describe his activities during an ordinary day from 1919 to 1936.

"He always arose no later than five o'clock and often before five o'clock in the morning. At half past five he joined the Community in meditation and at six o'clock he assisted at the Mass where he received Holy Communion. Then he heard another Mass as an act of grace.

"After a very light breakfast at seven o'clock, he rested and prayed in his room until nine. However, the Superior of the Oratory often sent for Brother André before nine o'clock to see visitors in great distress. From nine until noon he received the sick and other visitors in his office. He usually spoke with the visitors in a hushed voice difficult to understand. He prayed with some of them. He massaged others with the medal of Saint Joseph or simply with his hands, the men only. To certain of them he said, 'You are not sick. Leave your crutches, walk! Make such and such a movement of the afflicted limbs.'

"To others who came to him seeking counsel and light Brother André said they must make a novena on their rosaries or take Communion or say prayers in honor of the Holy Wounds of our Lord to obtain the favors they desired from Saint Joseph. He also recommended that they suffer in patience and read the Apostles, *The Imitation of Christ,* and the lives of the saints.

"After his office hours, at about a quarter of twelve, he would go to the particular examination. However, after 1925 (when he was eighty) his Superiors excused him from this exercise and also the other exercises of the rule.

"Having eaten a light luncheon, Brother André retired to his room for repose and prayer. Already there would be numerous visitors awaiting him. He pursued the same labors in the afternoon until five o'clock. Usually at five one of his friends, M. Pichette, M. Corbeil or M. Gadbois, a pharmacist, or others, all of whom were authorized by the Superior, would call for him and take him to visit the sick in their homes or the hospitals. I can say that the visits in general followed an itinerary drawn up by the Superior of the Oratory in accordance with requests which had been made to him. Usually Brother André took his evening meal with the family of his companion of that day.

"Brother André returned to the Oratory between nine and ten o'clock, after which he conducted his spiritual exercises, often with his companion in the Crypt of the Oratory, sometimes alone in his room.

"On Friday of each week Brother André did not ordinarily make home visits but remained at the Oratory for the Holy Hour and the Way of the Cross, which were held every week at the Oratory. Before going to bed Brother André ran all through the Crypt, shutting the windows, turning out the lights and making sure that everything was in order. I am not exactly sure when Brother André went to bed, but I believe it was not before eleven o'clock.

"To my knowledge this was the daily program of Brother André during the last thirty years of his life."

As his friends often observed, it was incredible that any man could perform so much physical activity on such a small amount of food. Brother Placide Vermandère, himself an ascetic, said that Brother André's diet of boiled lumps of dough was "completely unworthy. It would have made me ill." Only when he took his evening meal at such homes as the Pichettes' in their small cheerful kitchen with its white and red dimity curtains and big curlicue Victorian stove did he get any real nourishment.

The hours he spent in his office—his *bureau*—were a fearful drain on him. As he once said, "You do not go to the hospital unless you are sick," meaning that almost everyone who came to see him was suffering from some grave malady of the body or soul. He so dreaded the long hours in that bureau of tribulation that he would say in his punning way, "I am going to my *bourreau*" (my executioner).

Though the strain made him nervous and often irritable, it never soured Brother André's disposition. Brother Placide described his own experience with him to the writer.

"I first saw Brother André when, as a child, my parents took me over the mountain on foot to visit the Oratory," Brother Placide said. "I got to know him well much later when I was living in the community in my capacity as organist. Had I fore-seen the tremendous reputation he would have I would have paid closer attention, but he was just a confrere of mine whom I thought of as a saintly man. It is hard to think of a man as perfect when you live with him. I don't believe in saints with-out a touch of human frailty.

"Brother André more or less took to me. He often invited me to his room which was more or less a sanctuary. . . . There he showed me some of the letters he had received, the saddest I have ever read. He got hundreds of these letters every day. The poor people wrote to him freely, telling him their woes. Brother Hyacinth, his secretary, usually answered them in a general way unless one was especially difficult. He took these to Brother André.

"Yet, Brother André was very jolly with his friends. Some-times he pretended to fight with them, shadowboxing. Occa-sionally when he came home late he asked me to make the rounds with him shutting the windows of the Crypt. He was a very careful man and somewhat fearful of the dark. Then we would make the Stations of the Cross. Very slowly. When you are nineteen or twenty years old it seems so long a time. I would tire and sit in a pew waiting for him to finish.

"Looking back I feel that it was the greatest privilege of my life to have lived with him. I have the oil of Saint Joseph and believe that Brother André can help me. I have obtained favors for others, for people I know in Belgium, through him.

"If Brother André is not considered a saint I don't know who could be."

Brother André was not just foolishly timid in his anxiety about locking up the chapel and the Crypt. Once he received a crank letter threatening to plant a bomb in the Oratory.

On that occasion, not only the police, but his friends the fire-men rallied to the protection of the shrine. There were hun-dreds of firemen all over the mountain. Either no bombing had really been intended, or the crank dared not attempt to break through that cordon of stalwart men in blue.

However, the old chapel was robbed twice. The first time thieves broke in and stole about one hundred dollars in alms. On the second occasion they took two altar vases. This was a tremendous shock to Brother André since the money and vases belonged to Saint Joseph.

Even about such things Brother André sometimes joked. He walked into Monsieur Robert's shop one day and said, "The Oratory was robbed last night."

"Mon Dieu!" Robert exclaimed. "What did the thieves get?"

Brother André twinkled, "A bagful of miracles."

In questioning the Servant of God's heroic love of his neighbor the Promoter General of the Faith in Rome quoted testimony that Brother André was often cross with his visitors; that he was especially "brusque with women," that he "rapped his cane on his desk with a loud noise scaring them and sometimes making them cry." Father Clément said that he often had to console visitors whom Brother André had frightened. And Dr. Joseph Lionel Lamy, his personal physician, testified that Brother André was "sometimes sullen and very disagreeable."

Brother André's testiness in his last years was described in the testimony of his Superior, Father Cousineau, who said, "I know that Brother André had an extremely nervous temperament joined with excessive timidity. His face had a look of severity which vanished when he smiled. I think that many people, frightened by his ascetic visage and his energetic desire to cut short useless conversations, did not notice that Brother André, even in his brusque movements, retained a serene expression which was the image of his inner self."

These "brusque movements" were due in part to Brother André's great age and his high-strung nature, and also to the digestional difficulties which plagued him all his life. Virtually every witness spoke of his *"estomac capricieux."* Most of all it was due to his nervousness in the presence of women. His prudence and delicacy concerning the opposite sex was indeed heroic. He could not bear the thought of moral sin, and disliked even to say the words condemning it in his directory. For example, Brother Placide says, "In making the Way of the Cross, there is a sentence in the ritual referring to the 'The sting of concupiscence.' Brother André always stopped at that point—he would not say it. However, he was not prudish but prudent."

Yet all his life Brother André felt that he was subject to the temptations of the flesh as part of the running battle he fought with the demon. According to Father Cousineau's testimony, "About 1933, Brother André [aged seventy-eight] came to see me at Saint Laurent College where I was then Superior and asked me to pray for him. 'I have great temptations against chastity,' he told me. I also know that Father Labonté found Brother André prostrated in his room one day, and that he confided in Father Labonté that he was the prey of such violent temptations against chastity that he did not know where he was. . . . Father Labonté questioned him, and afterward enlightened and consoled him."

Azarias Claude, testifying on the subject of Brother André and his female visitors, said, "The women sometimes expressed surprise that Brother André refused to touch them or to rub them. They asked, 'Is there then danger in touching us?'

"Brother André answered humorously, 'Yes, it's poison.' "

Nothing upset the little brother so much as a woman who appeared in his office immodestly dressed. Then his expression became frighteningly stern and his wit biting. One lady who came to ask a favor carefully explained that she could not make much of a donation because she had very little money. Eying her fashionably short skirt Brother André said, "Yes, I see you are too poor to buy enough material to cover yourself properly."

The most remarkable of Brother André's encounters with

demanding women was also described before the Tribunal by M. Claude. This particular lady was very rich and pompous. She arrived in a limousine driven by a chauffeur, with another attendant on the box. According to M. Claude, "Her legs were so feeble that she had to be supported between two men."

Continuing his testimony he said, "Brother André gave her but a short interview and then rang his bell to mark the end of the audience. Well, that woman came out without having had time to explain at great length what she desired. She came out fuming against Brother André who had dismissed her so brusquely.

"The sick woman did not perceive that she had come out of Brother André's office without the help of her companions. Someone in the crowd said to her, 'You have no reason to complain. You are walking without help.'

"It was only then that the lady and her companions realized what had happened. All three of them burst into tears on understanding that the invalid now walked as easily as though she had never been ill."

There is no testimony, direct or indirect, as to just what were the "temptations of the flesh," which plagued Brother André. He was far too prudent to describe them except by that general phrase. One can therefore only draw conclusions from the character of the man himself. So gentle, so delicate and so innocent was he in every worldly matter that it seems impossible that they could have been as wicked as he imagined them to be. One is forced to conclude that the dark thoughts which troubled him so deeply were in reality as guiltless as the first faint recognition in a growing boy of his approaching manhood.

CHAPTER THIRTEEN

...And Great Joy

Iᴀ Brother André continued to have severe ordeals, he also had moments of great joy. One of these was the celebration at the Oratory in 1925 of his eightieth birthday. At the same time Father Dion celebrated his golden anniversary in the priesthood and Father Clément his twenty-fifth.

People began climbing the stairs to the Oratory, many of them on their knees, as early as six o'clock that morning. By eight thirty 25,000 people were packed solidly on the terraces and the roof of the Crypt. At nine His Excellency M. F. Fallon, Bishop of London, celebrated the Mass.

Then Father Edouard Laurin, C.S.C., spoke in the name of the community, saying, "These are the three artisans, ardent and indefatigable, of the cult of Saint Joseph . . . always we found them standing in the breach with neither pride nor weakness. They possess a treasure of piety, penitence and zeal. And their virtues bring down upon all of us who know them benedictions from on high. Long may they live for our joy and the greater glory of God! These are the wishes which we formulate here at the feet of Saint Joseph."

Afterward the three religious had their photographs taken together. Usually Brother André was very shy of photographers and when forced to pose for them wore a pained expression.

But this once, standing next to his Superior and his priest, who were also his dear friends, he wore a broad grin.

A gala dinner was served in the presbytery at noon. There is no record of the menu but one may hope that for once the little brother had a sumptuous repast. He spent the rest of the day in his office receiving his unhappy visitors.

Another sort of fete in which Brother André took great pleasure was the annual pilgrimage of the Catholic Workers' Syndicates in September. Ever since his own youthful days of hard labor, the little brother had had an especial softness in his heart for men who worked with their hands. And was not Saint Joseph their patron saint because he had been one of them?

These pilgrimages grew to great proportions. Even as early as 1922, Brother André had the happiness of seeing 20,000 Catholic workers climbing the mountain singing in the November dusk. Their progress was marked by flaring torches and thousands upon thousands of candles shielded in transparent, lily-like holders which lighted their earnest faces.

The most joyous thing that ever happened to Brother André is described in the testimony of several witnesses, among them Father Bergeron: "I can say that I learned from Father Emile Deguire the following fact. On the 28th of September, 1931, Brother André had gone to bed in his room at the Oratory. As he lay there his eyes were struck by the sight of a luminous heart which he believed to be that of our Lord Jesus Christ. A few moments later he saw the Virgin carrying the Infant Jesus in her arms. She advanced toward Brother André, who rose from his bed, saying, 'My Mother, my good Mother!'

"The next day Brother André reported the fact to Father Deguire who embodied it in a signed document."

The year 1929 was significant for the Oratory. Over two million pilgrims and visitors climbed the mountain. On November

19 the twenty-fifth anniversary of the founding of the Oratory was celebrated.

Despite his ninety-one years of age, Father Louis Geoffrion, who had celebrated the first Mass in the primitive chapel, insisted on coming out of retirement to say Mass at six thirty. He was assisted by Brother André, who was eighty-four years old.

At the same time Father Benjamin Lecavalier, who as Superior of the College of Notre Dame in 1904 had encouraged Brother André's work, celebrated the Mass in the first chapel. His assistant was that good workman who had built the primitive shrine, Brother Abundius. Afterward the Pontifical Mass was chanted by Cardinal R. M. Rouleau, Archbishop of Quebec.

In 1930 came the Great Depression, which diminished the stream of pilgrims for a while and slowed the work of the basilica. During those years of material misfortune Brother André was busier than ever doing what he could to alleviate individual misery.

However, to those who were not actually in dire distress he usually said, "Money is nothing. You ought to be worrying about your soul. You might lose it as well."

Despite the difficulties of the times Brother André was never happier. For he was encouraged on all sides. In 1926, Father Roy had been elevated to be assistant to the Superior General of Holy Cross, and his place at the Oratory had been taken by Father Clément. Thus the priest who had once been too blind to read his breviary was now the Superior of a great and growing organization for the promotion of the faith and the cult of Saint Joseph.

In those last years the cures came ever more frequently. Even some of Brother André's old antagonists, the doctors of Montreal, ceased to plague him and went so far as to encourage his visits to their patients. They began to testify to his cures, and even called on him to help them in distress. Dr. Lamy testified:

"To my knowledge Brother André operated some extraordinary cures.

"Well, one evening Dr. Dufresne was very disturbed about the condition of his wife and telephoned Brother André. He told Brother André that Mme. Dufresne had not slept for a long time. Brother André responded on the telephone to Dr. Dufresne, 'Your wife is asleep now.'

"The doctor interrupted the conversation to go and check on the state of his wife. He found her in deep sleep."

This new attitude of the doctors was true of Protestants as well as Catholics. Léopold Lussier says, "In the Catholic hospitals we visited they held to the letter of the rule about visiting hours. Brother André had to leave with the others at eight thirty in the evening. But the head doctor of one Protestant hospital said, "That man can come to see my patients at any hour of the day or night."

As may be seen from this, Brother André did not reserve his ministrations or his cures to Catholics alone. He received and visited people of all faiths or none. M. Claude testified: "As to heretics, schismatics and also unbelievers, Brother André treated them with more kindness and sympathy than the Catholics. He wanted to gain the confidence of such people. When the right time came he talked to them of the goodness of God, of religion. In answer to Question Fifty I have already reported how Brother André cured a Protestant in Howick. The Protestant came voluntarily to see Brother André and had confidence in him. He profited by the visits of Protestants and unbelievers to slide in a good word to them, an evangelical word."

On this same subject Salvatore Marotta, a successful businessman of Montreal who often drove Brother André, testified: "An American from Los Angeles, California, who was suffering from cancer came to Saint Joseph's Oratory. I saw him and talked with him. He was a Freemason and wore the insignia on his lapel. When he presented himself at Brother André's office, the porter saw his Masonic insignia but let him in anyway.

"Brother André asked him the reason for his visit and the American said that he had an intestinal cancer which caused him terrible pain. Brother André advised him to rub himself with Saint Joseph's medal and oil, which the sick man did.

"Immediately after this rubbing the man returned to see Brother André, telling him with cries of joy that his intestinal pains had disappeared, that he was cured.

"I do not know if this man showed a desire to be converted. I do know that he was very grateful to Brother André for his cure.

"The porter remarked to Brother André, 'So you cure Free-masons.'

"Brother André replied to him, 'Notice that this man came a long way to Saint Joseph's Oratory, that he took six days and six nights for his journey. His Masonic insignia is nothing but a piece of tin, but there was great confidence in his heart and that is what matters.' "

Brother André only had three illnesses serious enough to keep him from his work. According to Father Cousineau he suffered from influenza in 1918, acute gastritis in 1931 and pneumonia in 1932. M. Pichette described the beginning of the latter illness: "One night I went to his room in the Oratory and knocked on the door. There was no answer but I could hear him breathing heavily with a rasping sound. I knocked again. He opened the door and stood holding himself erect by clinging to the bedpost and the door of his shower. He looked half dead.

" 'You are sick,' I said.

"He nodded feebly and I said, 'Why not come to my home for a good rest?'

"In a voice that was no more than a whisper he answered, 'I cannot go without permission. Please ask the Superior.' Then he smiled at me.

"I went to Father Clément and told him of Brother André's request. 'He is too sick to be moved,' the Superior said.

[149]

" 'But he smiled when I asked him to come home with me.'

" 'If you could make him smile in the state he is in, take him by all means.' Father Clément said.

"So I bundled Brother André up in many blankets and took him to my house."

M. Pichette's home was the top floor of a small suburban house. You came up a flight of steep wooden stairs to the kitchen, the sunny cheerful room where Brother André had so many happy meals. Each room of the apartment contained one or more holy objects or shrines. In the small, stiffly furnished parlor, Baby Jesus lay in a wooden cradle. The Virgin in her blue robes with a long jeweled necklace stood on the mantelpiece, and in a corner was Saint Joseph all in white. In another room was a statuette of the Savior which Brother André had given M. Pichette, and in a central position was a tiny sliver of wood believed to be a relic of the True Cross.

Brother André was given the best bedroom, where he slept in a big double brass bed. There was a statuette of St. Joseph on a table and holy pictures on all the walls. Two big windows looked out on the small garden which he loved so well. The whole apartment was thus redolent of the simple piety of the Pichettes. Brother André always felt very serene and at home in that place.

However, on this occasion he did not recuperate as he usually did, and after a week Doctor Lamy said he must go to the great hospital called the Hotel-Dieu. He was there for twenty days. According to Father Cousineau's testimony, "Sister Le Royer of the Hotel-Dieu affirmed to me that during his illness Brother André left a truly edifying memory of patience and Christian piety, and of zeal to resume his devotion to Saint Joseph.

"Also, Sister Le Royer told Brother André her troubles and Brother André recommended that she write them down and place them at the foot of the statue of Saint Joseph. She reported to me that Brother André advised her with so much conviction to have recourse to Saint Joseph that she felt that her confidence in Saint Joseph and her devotion to Saint Joseph gained a vital impetus.

"While at the Hotel-Dieu Brother André told Monsieur [l'Abbé] Joseph Nelson Duquette that he had seen on the wall of his room an eye which reminded him of those which one sees on certain holy pictures from which stream rays of light that illumine the image of the Holy Virgin or Saint Joseph. Brother André was greatly moved by this vision from which he derived the meaning that, 'The more one suffers, the closer one is to God.'

"Monsieur l'Abbé Duquette affirmed this to me with great emotion under oath."

The only thing which troubled Brother André's nurses was his refusal to eat proper food. According to Father Cousineau, "Sister Le Royer reported to me that during all three of Brother André's illnesses she had great difficulty making him eat. He would accept nothing but wheat flour softened in [hot] water and seasoned with salt. One day Sister Le Royer said to him, 'But is it glue that you wish?'

" 'Yes,' replied Brother André, 'it is glue.' "

After he was discharged from the hospital well but very weak, the Superior ordered Brother André to go to the Pichettes' for a rest. He stayed a whole month with these devoted friends. At the end of that time he was completely recovered.

Though Brother André had only three major illnesses, he was never really well. Doctor Lamy testified that "From 1928 on I was Brother André's personal physician. He always suffered from digestive troubles which brought about a secondary impairment of his liver. He was obliged to follow a very strict diet and for considerable periods could digest nothing but liquids. . . . His symptoms included headaches, vertigo, nausea, distended stomach and intestinal disorders.

"When Brother André felt himself particularly unwell, he would send for me, if his Superior judged it advisable. On these occasions I found him in bed, almost always dressed in his soutane and enveloped by many blankets surmounted by a heavy overcoat. Brother André did not take many medicines. He accepted them, but rarely took them, on the pretext that he was feeling better."

Anyone who has suffered the misery of a temporarily upset stomach must wonder how Brother André managed to go cheerily on through his seventeen- or eighteen-hour day, comforting, counseling and curing the sick, while he himself was in a worse case than many of his petitioners. It was indeed heroic fortitude, as much a work of faith as the braces and crutches lining the walls of the Crypt, or the great church in honor of Saint Joseph rising slowly on the mountain.

On Brother André's ninety-first birthday, August 9, 1936, it seemed that half the world paid tribute to him. Papers all over Canada and the United States carried the news in headlines and many of them sent reporters to interview him. He was still extraordinarily active, perhaps agile is the exact word. A reporter for the Boston *Evening American* who interviewed him in his office wrote:

> He stands so small, about five feet tall, that you can hardly see him over the top of his counter. While I sat in his office talking to him, suddenly, with the quickness of a monkey, he leaped on a chair and from there to a nearby radiator-top, and was busily winding a grandfather's clock. You'd never believe to see him looking a little bit pleased with himself that he had celebrated his ninety-first birthday on Sunday.

Through the reporters he sent a message to the people of Canada's great neighbor: "The United States is ever in my prayers. Always I pray for everyone in America. She must have faith; even more faith. When chaos prevails in the world we, each one of us, are to blame. We are lacking in faith."

Then came his final word to the faithful which held a premonition as well as a message: "Always be prepared to die! We think least of the most important thing that is to happen to us."

[152]

Walls and a Roof

THERE were certain things left that Brother André felt impelled to do. There was most of all the building of the basilica. Work on it had temporarily ceased for lack of funds. The high walls stood on the mountainside open to the sky like a lovely ruin unroofed by age, and more melancholy for never having been completed. The great dome which was to stir faithful hearts by its majesty was no more than a sketch on a drawing board whose fulfillment seemed indefinitely postponed. One of the architects who had conceived it, M. Venne, was dead, and his partner had no heart to continue the firm. Everything was at a standstill.

In this situation the Council of the Oratory met on the first Wednesday of November, 1936. It was now headed by a new Superior. In 1934, Father Clément had retired to be succeeded by Father Alfred Charron, who in 1936, was followed by Father Albert Cousineau.

The new Superior was a priest of the modern school, which was dear to the heart of Pius XII, himself the most future-minded Pope. He was an energetic man with short-clipped brown hair and quick, intelligent eyes behind rimless spectacles. Though his love of God and devotion to Saint Joseph were as fervent as those of the most austere mystic of the old days, he followed Pope Pius' belief that the Universal Church must be flexible as to means, while holding fast to eternal truth and basic principle. Modern invention must be utilized to the full in the service of God. Thus it is better to ride than to walk and to fly than to ride if thereby the works of faith are speeded up and multiplied. Father Cousineau, who is now Bishop of Cap Haitien, was also a man of tremendous enthusiasms; the greatest of these being for Brother André and the work of the Oratory.

Well might he cherish his aged confrere; for his own nephew had been cured by Brother André. The child had set himself on fire playing with a box of matches. He was taken in a critical condition to the Hospital of Notre-Dame-de-l'Espérance at Saint Laurent where Father Cousineau went to see him. As Father Cousineau told the Tribunal, "The child was in such pain that he could not bear the touch of the dressings on his wounds without screaming and crying. I decided to ask Brother André to see him. I was not present, but the nurse, Sister Marie de Saint Camille of the Sisters of Hope, and the parents of the child were witnesses to the visit of Brother André. The child, who could not bear the dressings, permitted his wound to be rubbed by Brother André without complaining. The nurses continued the dressings and the child was soon able to leave the hospital. Brother André had said to the child, 'Fear nothing, you will be cured.'

"The Sisters of the hospital told me that they considered the case desperate."

There was very little for Father Cousineau to get enthusiastic about on that dreary November day in 1936. Father Bergeron, who was present, tells how the Council debated the question of what to do. All of them were desperately anxious to speed the work, not only for the sake of Saint Joseph, but also for Brother André. They could see that the little brother whom they loved so well had failed noticeably since his birthday. The Superior and all his confreres hoped that he might live to see the great dome crowning the work of which he was the chief artisan.

The talk in the council room of the presbytery went around and around. No one could think of a practical solution. The principle originally laid down by Archbishop Bruchési that the Work of the Oratory must be financed by free gifts from the faithful forbade their making a special drive for money. The duty of prudence prevented them from risking a fresh start before the money was in hand. There was apparently no way to go on.

Brother André, as usual, sat quietly in his place listening and saying nothing. When they had talked themselves into an impasse, he spoke: "We all want to cover the basilica as soon as possible. Let us put a statue of Saint Joseph within its unfinished walls. He will soon find a roof for himself!"

Bergeron says, "That same day after luncheon we went to pray at the primitive Oratory. Then reciting the Rosary we set ourselves to climb the rugged slope to the basilica. Brother André tried to follow the procession but stopped exhausted. A poignant sadness, a tightness squeezed our hearts, as amid the joy of our gesture of faith the same thought came to all of us; that the basilica would be completed, but its builder, Brother André, would no longer be among us."

Brother André sat on a rock with his worn old heart pumping crazily while he watched the procession file through the gaping entrance of the basilica. Then two strong young religious came running back, and between them carried him up "the steep, unfinished cement stairs until they gained the cluttered nave with its monstrous topless columns." There he stood looking up through the scaffolding at the gray autumnal clouds trailing their scarves of mist over the unfinished walls.

Father Bergeron continues: "The statue of Saint Joseph was placed in the apse. In the midst of our prayers we were suddenly aware of the grandeur of the work already realized on Mount Royal. It seemed to us that the venerable man had been truly inspired when he proposed the act which we were performing. For it was a repetition, forty years later, of his own gesture of placing the first statuette in a shelter formed by the rocks."

That night Brother André may have had his last bout with the devil. At other times he had been quite certain when the fiend attacked him; as many witnesses avowed. For example Monsieur Antonio Valente testified: "Brother André told me ... that he often fought with the devil at night. He told me that when the demon came, he heard a noise of chains. But he said he had no fear of the devil, that he had often beaten him fighting body to body."

However this time Brother André thought that perhaps it was a dream. He gave a cry in the night that brought Brother Osée rushing into his room. He found Brother André clutching his throat unable to speak. When he had recovered a little he said, "Perhaps I dreamed it, but my throat hurts terribly. I think the devil was choking me." Then Brother André grinned, "I guess he doesn't want a roof on the basilica. But I said to him, 'Don't you think one might desire death so that one might go to see the good God?' That ended it. He fled."

The results of the communal act of faith were rapidly apparent. Father Cousineau got permission from the Superior General of Holy Cross and obtained the approval of Bishop Gauthier to attempt a loan of $1,200,000 to roof the basilica and complete the dome. The money was easily raised. At the same time a new and inspired architect was found to carry on the work. He was Dom Paul Bellot, a French Benedictine, who for this purpose associated himself with two Canadian architects, Messieurs Parent and Tourville.

The original plans had envisaged a traditional Renaissance interior for the great basilica. Dom Bellot's imagination soared beyond the conventional to combine the austere lines of modern architecture at its best with the dignity of the Renaissance style. Instead of cluttered columns the great trigonal roof was to be supported by high geometric arches springing from pilasters set against the walls of the nave. The dome was to be raised; this would give it a lofty grace. Since this would make the interior unsymmetrical a false ceiling was designed to mask the tremendous height of the outer dome. When Brother André saw the new plans he was well pleased.

However well things appeared to be going, Brother André was not one to leave every burden on the shoulders of Saint Joseph. Soon after placing the statue in the unfinished nave he requested the permission of the Superior to pay his annual visit to the United States. This time he had a very ambitious project in mind; no less than a trip to New York to interest the Rockefellers in giving funds for the basilica.

Father Cousineau was greatly troubled by this request, for he thought the little brother too feeble for such a journey. But so ardent was Brother André's spirit, and so absolute his conviction that he would find the strength, that his Superior yielded. For Father Cousineau was by now convinced that Brother André's proposals were, in truth, divinely inspired.

Arrangements for the visit were made by Mme. Laporte, who telephoned her friend, Miss Mary Ryan, in New York to ask if Brother André could stay at the Ryans' apartment. Miss Ryan's reaction to the suggestion was decidedly mixed. On one hand she was delighted by the honor of having such a holy man stay in her family's home; at the same time she was terrified by the responsibility of caring for this frail ancient, whom she regarded as a saint.

"What does he eat?" she asked feebly.

"That need not worry you," Mme. Laporte said. "Just have some crusts of bread and plenty of black coffee."

Brother André traveled alone on the night train to New York. Miss Ryan and her father met him at the station, and drove him up Fifth Avenue. It was a cold, bright, winter morning. People were scurrying along the sidewalks, but the heavy traffic on the avenue proceeded at a crawl-and-stop pace. Brother André peered up at the gleaming buildings and smiled at the gay shop windows.

"How do you like New York?" Miss Ryan asked.

Her small guest twinkled at her. "It's much too slow for me," he said.

Brother André was touched to find a statuette of Saint Joseph and a beautiful model of the shrine at Lourdes in his room. His delight was so genuine that Miss Ryan's anxieties, which had reached a peak just before the train pulled in, were considerably allayed. However she was still anxious about the little dinner party she had planned that night. For one thing she had abandoned the crusts-of-bread menu in favor of a thick steak, and she had invited four priestly friends to meet her famous guest.

She need not have worried. The little brother felt tremendously honored by the presence of the priests, and was at his merriest. When the steak was passed he gave one quizzical look at his hostess and helped himself to a large piece. He even ate some of the dessert, which was entirely contrary to his habit. The fact is that Brother André was instinctively too courteous to embarrass his hostess by refusing the food she had provided. Fortunately his *estomac* was not in the least *capricieux* that evening.

In fact, Brother André had not overestimated his strength. He felt unusually well during the three days he was with the Ryans, and they were one of the happiest times of his life. The one disappointment was that Mr. Rockefeller was out of town, but Mr. John Burke gave him a fat check for the Oratory as a consolation prize.

Early in the morning of the second day of his visit the Ryans took Brother André to Mass in the Church of Saint Francis of Assisi. The beautiful little church and the piety of the congregation moved him to say, "There is great love and devotion here. I feel it all through me."

The mountain transformed. The new Oratory begins to take shape in 1923.

Brother André among his friends and helpers, firemen from Station 27.

On Brother André's 80th birthday, with two other "artisans of the faith," Father Dion, on his golden anniversary in the priesthood, Father Clément, on his twenty-fifth anniversary.

Brother André's last portrait. (Photograph by Armand.)

January, 1937, Brother André, in the Crypt in the Oratory, amid the crutches of the many who had come to the shrine and left them behind.

Rome, July, 1950: The testimony of the Cause in charge of a Swiss Guard, and (from left to right) Father Edward L. Heston (later Postulator), Father Alfred Laplante, the Very Reverend Father Albert Cousineau, Superior of Saint Joseph's Oratory, and the late Monsignor René Fontenelle.

The Oratory of Saint Joseph with visitors and celebrants at the fête of the Sacred Heart, June 15, 1958.

The crowded nave of the Basilica.

Paul-Émile Cardinal Léger saying mass on June 15, 1958.

The second station of the cross on the Oratory hillside, sculpture by
Louis Parent. (Photograph by Marcel Cognac.)

After that he visited a hospital where, among other patients, he saw the child of friends of the Ryans, who had acute mastoiditis. As he gently rubbed the little boy's ears the pain went away, and he and the child laughed together in happiness. There is no record as to whether the cure was permanent.

Less fortunate was one woman whom he could not help. With her he talked about the beauties of paradise. He told Miss Ryan about it afterward: "She listened to me," he said to his hostess, "but then she said, 'All the same, Brother, we all fear death.'

"I told her that when one has led a good life, death is not a thing to fear, for it is the gate of heaven. And she said, 'Of course! And yet the sky is very far away!'

"In reply I recited "Our Father" in a whisper and then I said to her, 'You know the good God heard me—and that shows we are very close to heaven.' "

When the time came to put Brother André on the train for Providence, where he was going to see his sister, Mary Ryan gave him her most precious possession, a first-class relic of the Little Flower, "To guard you on your travels."

"I have Saint Joseph's medal," he said half eager and half unwilling to accept the gift.

"Take it please, anyhow," she said.

As she put it in his hand he said boyishly, "Is it really a first-class relic?"

"Yes, here are the papers that prove it."

Pushing his spectacles up on his broad, bald forehead and putting his nose within four inches of the paper, Brother André slowly read the document. Then overflowing with happiness, he boarded the train.

When Brother André returned from his trip everybody remarked how much better he looked. Father Clément said, "You were right in saying you would live to see your basilica."

"I never said I would see it *finished*," Brother André replied

What Throne of Glory

On Christmas Eve, 1936, Brother André made his rounds of hospitals and homes as usual. His final visit was to the home of the Laportes to tell them about his trip to New York. There was so much to tell that he stayed for a long time, talking with such animation that a little color warmed his transparent skin and his eyes danced behind his spectacles. The Laportes thought he had not looked so well in years.

At midnight Mass Brother André was back at the Oratory sitting in his inconspicuous pew on the Epistle side of the Crypt. He assisted at the first two Masses during which were said prayers for Pope Pius XI who was desperately ill and believed to be dying. In the midst of the third Mass Brother André was so overcome by fatigue, dizziness and a burning fever that he asked Brother Osée to help him to his room. There was quite a stir at the unusual sight of this devoted man leaving the Crypt during Mass, but his confreres were reassured by the look of happiness on his face.

After the Mass his old friend Father Clément came to see him. He was lying on his narrow bed still dressed in his clean, patched soutane. "What made you look so radiant as you left the Crypt?" Father Clément asked.

"I was thinking that in a year or two Christmas Mass will be celebrated in the basilica."

[163]

"You will be there to assist at it, Brother."

"This is the last Christmas that I shall be here below. The Pope will not die, it is I who will die in his place," Brother André said cheerfully. (Pius XI lived until 1939.)

"We need your help," Father Clément said.

"My work is done," Brother André replied. "And anyhow, if one can do things here, just think of how much more he can do in heaven."

The day after Christmas Father Cousineau asked Dr. Lamy to visit Brother André. The doctor testified that he diagnosed his illness as "a little grippe," and ordered him to remain in bed. Later acute gastric enteritis developed. At first Brother André was able to take care of himself, but presently he grew weaker. Brother Placide was assigned to nurse him. Before the Tribunal Brother Placide told of this: "I can say that I took care of Brother André during his last illness. I passed the greater part of three days and especially the nights in his room. As I remember, the Superior of the Oratory, Father Cousineau, said to me, 'I would be pleased if you would arrange your time so that you can watch over Brother André.'

"At first no one thought that Brother André was in his last illness, as far as I could tell. He seemed to me to be suffering and he spoke very little. If I remember rightly he asked me several times to rub his breast with his medal of Saint Joseph. He did not complain, but appeared to be praying.

"He was stretched out on his bed still wearing his soutane. I remember getting down on my knees beside his bed, perhaps to say a little prayer, perhaps more easily to understand Brother André if he needed anything. I do not recall exactly why, but I do remember that when he perceived that I was kneeling Brother André protested and made me get up. I have a feeling that Brother André understood that I had knelt out of respect for him. When I assured him that I was kneeling to understand him better, he appeared more tranquil."

During the last days of December Brother André got no

[164]

better and no worse. He appeared to be suspended between life and death on a scale that might move either way. On the afternoon of December 31, Father Cousineau and Father Charron, who was Superior Provincial of Holy Cross, consulted with Dr. Lamy. He testified: "They asked me whether, in view of the New Year's Day visits which Brother André would inevitably receive if he stayed at the Oratory, and also in view of the state of his health which necessitated special care which he could not get in the infirmary of the community, what would be the best course to follow. Would it be better to send him to a hospital or to take the risk of keeping him at Saint Joseph's Oratory? I immediately chose the hospital, and made sure that the authorities of the little hospital run by the Sisters of Hope at Saint Laurent had a room for Brother André. The Superior left it to me to decide the question of the hospital.

"After making the arrangements I went to Brother André to tell him of our decision and induce him to accept it. At first I evaded telling him that a room was already reserved at the Saint Laurent Hospital.

"First I pointed out to him that the next day, the first of January, would be very tiring because of the customary visits. Then I said, 'How would you like to hide yourself someplace?'

"Smiling he acquiesced in this project. I suggested the Hotel-Dieu, which did not seem to please him.

" 'What would you say,' I asked him, 'to a little corner in the Saint Laurent Hospital?'

"His face became radiant at the suggestion and he agreed completely."

Father Cousineau then came to see his confrere and tell him officially that he must go to the hospital. Though he does not say so in his testimony, Father Cousineau was terribly worried. His devotion to Brother André was so great that the normal relationship of superior to lay brother might almost have been reversed had it not been for the discipline of the order which both men respected and obeyed.

[165]

The ambulance arrived between eight and nine that evening. Brother André was carefully wrapped in so many blankets that he was quite lost. Only his wrinkled brown face was visible to his saddened confreres who stood looking down at the stretcher in which he lay. He grinned up at them and said, "I look like somebody going to the North Pole."

Brother Placide rode with him to the hospital. He testified: "I accompanied Brother André on the journey in the ambulance. I remember that they had bundled him in a great many warm coverings to guard against a chill. Brother André, bundled up like that and fastened to the stretcher by tight straps, asked me several times to loosen him lest he suffocate. I encouraged him to have patience, saying that we would soon arrive."

So they brought Brother André to the narrow, white woodenwalled room at Saint Laurent.

The next day, New Year's Day, 1937, Father Cousineau came to visit his little brother. He found him lying contentedly in the white iron bedstead. Before the Tribunal the Superior said, "When I asked him if he suffered greatly he replied, 'Yes, I am suffering, but I thank God for according me the grace of suffering, for I have so great a need of it.' And he added, 'One does not think enough about death.' "

As his Superior sat beside the bed comforting him, the saintly little brother made a touching acknowledgment of his humble awareness of his human frailty. Father Cousineau testified, "It was then that he said to me, 'I have something to ask of you. Pray for my conversion.' "

Brother André's nurse at Saint Laurent was Sister Marie de Saint Camille of the Sisters of Hope. She told the Tribunal: "I wish to say that I have great confidence in the intercession of Brother André because I was his nurse for seven days and I noted many extraordinary things about him. Before that I was somewhat skeptical about the efficacy of Brother André's visits, not that I lacked confidence in the virtue of this religious, but I did not see the need for this ancient one to discommode himself by coming to see the sick. One could as well have just asked him to pray for the sick.

"However, when Brother André fell into the final coma visitors were permitted to approach him and I was astounded by the great number of visitors who came close to Brother André and touched his clothes or belongings. I interpreted this as a manifestation of a great faith in the virtue of Brother André among all those people. During that time thousands of people . . . passed before Brother André, day and night. . . .

"They brought Brother André in an ambulance from Saint Joseph's Oratory. I remember that he was wearing his complete costume as a religious including his clerical collar. . . .

"At the beginning Brother André was able to drink by himself, but I noticed that he did so with great difficulty because his hand trembled. I hazarded an offer to help him. He accepted.

"I had heard that Brother André was very reserved and distant with women. I was a little embarrassed when I said to him: 'My Brother, I must now make your toilet.' Brother André accepted quite simply. With another sister I bathed his face and hands and rubbed his back. He accepted, murmuring, 'This must be very humiliating for you, Sister.'

"Then I asked, 'My Brother, what may I prepare for you to eat?' He answered, 'Boil some water. Mix a little flour and salt in water, and then dump it in the boiling water, stirring it so as to make a little gruel.'

"The first time I used cornstarch because it was milder. When I served him, Brother André said with slight malice, 'My Sister, that is not flour you put in here.'

"I admitted that it was cornstarch. The cornstarch seemed to upset him. After that I made the flour gruel six or seven times following Brother André's instructions. And strangely, this stuff that I called paste, this unappetizing mélange, Brother André appeared to enjoy and his stomach retained it.

"On the morning of January 2, Brother André declared that his right arm had become very painful. . . . In the absence of Dr. Lamy I asked the Father Rector of the Oratory [Cousineau] to send a substitute. The Rector suggested Dr. Joseph-Michel Badeaux of the town of Saint Laurent. He came to see the invalid and prescribed oxygen and injections of a mild sedative. Brother André slept for about an hour. When he awoke he said, smiling, to the doctor, 'I think the sister has given me a sedative. One can't trust these sisters.'

"In front of me Brother André had said to the doctor, 'Do not give me drugs.' We understood him to mean that he did not want morphine and we respected his wish.

"One time when I was helping him to eat he said, 'You have a vocation of patience,' to which I replied, 'Not like yours.' It was then that Brother André said, 'If only people would tell me what they want right off it would be much less tiring, but after all they have so much misery.'

"He was very patient. His only plaint was, 'My God, how I suffer!' He did not seem worried about anything. He said many times that he had more faith in prayer than pills.

"And many times he said, 'Heaven is so beautiful that it is worth all the trouble with which one prepares for it.'"

Brother André's arm grew worse. He had, in fact, suffered a slight stroke and the paralyzed limb pained him terribly.

"Why do you not ask Saint Joseph to heal you?"

"I can do nothing for myself," he answered.

Then they knew that the end was approaching.

Father Cousineau, who spent almost all his time at the hospital, wrote a beautiful account of Brother André's last few days. There is no fact in it to which he did not later testify under oath. But before the Tribunal, the Superior spoke in a dry, matter-of-fact manner because he knew that the judges might be prejudiced by a show of emotion. In his short article in *The Annals of Saint Joseph,* written at the moment of great loss, there is no such restraint. Because it reflects the sorrow and exaltation of Father Cousineau and those other confreres and friends of Brother André who gathered at his bedside and filled the corridors of the primitive little hospital, it is in a sense more truthful than his sworn testimony. For this reason it was embodied in the *Appendix Responsio* of the official record of the Cause, and will be quoted here:

Brother André has died. . . . Brother André is dead! . . . The grand artisan of Mount Royal is no more. It is a great bereavement. The bereavement of a people, the bereavement of the people!

His death was foretold. Brother André had a presentiment of his death. Already at the end of October, he said to Monsieur Chartier [the sculptor], who was executing a bust of him, that he was ready to leave this world. At the hospital, after one of the crises which buffeted him, he said with a serenity that was thrilling to the sisters at his bedside, "The Great Almighty is coming!" He seemed to savor the thought.

At another time he declared that all the doctors' remedies were now useless because the good God did not wish to help him. Why? he asked himself; and found the answer that he sought in calm acceptance of the will of God.

He smiled in the face of death. Was he discouraged? On the contrary, until the end he kept that faint smile of his, that slightly teasing smile which gave such charm to his conversation. He said to the sisters, whom he had to call for help more often than he liked, "It's your old nuisance who rings again!"

His arm was stricken; little by little the paralysis crept down it. In telling the nurses about it, the Brother said, "My arm is a Communist. He makes me suffer. The spiteful fellow will not let me alone." And the Brother laughed so heartily that his whole body shook, as he used to laugh when he was in good health. . . .

He offered his life willingly to God. According to the measure of his suffering Brother André gathered himself together and looked upon death with great gravity. When he said to me, "Pray for my conversion," that was his first great offering, for he accepted the coming of death as atonement for his sins. And he wished us to know that this was how he felt. Other matters disturbed him to the depths of his heart. We felt that he wanted to offer his life for the Successor of Saint Peter. He wanted to know about the Pope—"Does our Holy Father suffer much?" he asked. And in one of his last conscious moments here below he said to the sister at his bedside, "My hand is swollen. I am paralyzed like the Pope!"

He also prayed and worried about the troubles in Spain of which he talked seriously. Nor was his Community forgotten in his last moments. But the thought which occupied him most was his work at the Oratory. Twice he said in unequivocal words . . . "It will go forward, the temple of Saint Joseph will be completed!"

The thing which the guardians of Brother André's last hours admired most in the final moments before the great silence of his coma was the grateful joy which welled up in his heart. . . .

At eleven o'clock in the evening of January fourth, in the midst of the terrible pain which seized him, he breathed forth, in a hymn of love, his faith in the power and the charity of God. And he, who was always so silent about the work of the Oratory, felt a need to speak of the blessings that had been accorded on Mount Royal at the feet of Saint Joseph.

"You do not know," he said with fervor to the religious who redoubled their efforts to ease his pains, "you do not know all the blessings which the good God gave at the Oratory. . . . What misery there is in the world! I was in a position to know. I had to be lawyer, doctor, priest. But the good God helped. . . . Look you at the power of the good God!" And he told how Saint Joseph had cured one person of a tubercular hip, and how a paralytic was able to walk to the Benediction of the Blessed Sacrament; and how he had sent a sinner to confession. "See you the power of the good God!" he repeated with fervor. "How good God is! How beautiful! He must be beautiful for our soul is only a gleam of His beauty, and how lovely *it* is."

Then his suffering became even greater and as he grew more feeble his heart mounted in this prayer, an appeal for help from the Virgin whom he also loved so well: "Oh Mary, my sweet Mother and Mother of my sweet Savior, be kind to me and succor me!"

He halted for an instant and then went on softly, "Saint Joseph . . ." the other words were lost.

During the three hours more before he entered that state of coma which is the neighbor of death he repeated a cry at once supplicant and resigned: "How I suffer! My God! My God!"

After that the great silence. . . .

Father Cousineau was called to his Brother's bedside the next morning to administer Extreme Unction. The Superior General and many other priests and brothers and friends of Brother André, who crowded in to that small room and filled the corridor, assisted at the supreme sacramental prayer.

Father Cousineau wrote:

With our hearts overflowing with tears we followed the terrible combat that disease waged against the frail but indomitable nature of the dear servant of Saint Joseph—a nature accustomed to deprive itself of everything to battle against all satisfactions, to enfold itself in all humility, that which Saint Paul calls the mature man.

An alert—after twenty hours the disease triumphs. About eleven-thirty an alarm reunited confreres and friends who awaited in anguish the hour set by God to recompense the dear religious. Three doctors were at his bedside, prodigal of their care. The whole assemblage prayed together ardently. It was that most beautiful of prayers "Depart O Christian Soul"—the litany of the dying. And the litanies of Saint Joseph, the supplication for a happy death escaped all our lips with such piety as evoked in us the thought that he who dies repeats them for each of us, for all Christians, his brothers.

The last agony—calm returned again to the august invalid. For a moment we thought that God might leave us our dear Brother André. It was a vain hope. A few minutes later the battle was more violently renewed. It is half after midnight.

This is indeed the last agony. The sick man collapses, and we resume our prayers. I do not know what serenity filled that humble chamber of the Hospital of Saint Laurent where our dear Brother had been treated with such kindness and love. It was supernatural—the joy of one of the Elect who nears his recompense—who is taken away at last. The grateful prayer of the *Magnificat* mounted toward heaven. Thanks be to God for having given us Brother André; Thanks be to God for the grace accorded to His faithful servant, and by him to us.

What power was inherent in that prayer of the Virgin before the bed of pain which was already transformed into I know not what throne of glory!

Death—and now it is the end. A great effort and with an assuaging serenity, death has taken him who soothed so many miseries, physical and moral, who dried so many tears and eased so many burdens. It is fifty minutes after midnight.

We weep. Ours is not the sadness of despair; it is like a homesickness for heaven which overwhelmed us at that moment. After the *De Profundis,* we fervently recited the *Te Deum* of thankfulness. . . .

CHAPTER SIXTEEN

"Little Brother,

We Shall Miss You"

As soon as the Servant of God died, did the public spread the news that a saint had passed away? Did the people show him great devotion, and how did they manifest it?

Acclaim, veneration and adulating crowds of people were part of the ordinary routine of Brother André's later life. They never exalted his opinion of himself; for he thought of them as tributes not to him but to Saint Joseph. In his own mind he was still the humble and unworthy disciple, the transmission wire to and from Saint Joseph.

Yet, though in life he had known the pious regard of multitudes of people, Brother André would have been astounded by the tremendous outpouring of grief and adulation that followed his death. Again and again Father Bergeron calls it an apotheosis, and Brother Placide wrote: "Those of us who have lived those days of apotheosis and grace will remember them until the day of our death."

The seven days beginning January 6, 1937, were among the vilest of a Canadian winter. Snow, sleet, rain and fog alternated in dismal sequence, while the streets of Montreal were alternately morasses of slush and ribbons of treacherous ice. Yet nothing could keep the people from paying their final tribute to the man whom they loved and whom they thought of as a saint walking among them.

The churches of Montreal had been full of people praying for Brother André's recovery until the moment his death was announced. Then it seemed that all those people and many more came through the stormy weather to visit their little Brother. It was decided that, out of respect, his body would not be embalmed even though it was to be exposed for a week for the veneration of the faithful. During the morning of January 6 it remained at Saint Laurent, while thousands of people filed past it; touching it with their hands or with some religious object that they believed his virtue would sanctify. The priests and religious who came touched it with their crucifixes and religious medals.

On that grim, cold afternoon Brother André was brought back to the Oratory followed by his confreres and friends, while the church bells clanged their grief. According to Father Bergeron, "As the procession approached Mount Royal it became a triumph as a whole people seemed to join it for the solemn entrance to the Crypt."

Brother André was placed in the chapel opposite the great central doorway of the church which had been built by his devotion. Lying there on the white satin lining of his little wooden coffin with his black soutane and parchment-wrinkled face, his Superior's crucifix still on his breast, he looked so tiny to have aroused so great a tide of devotion. The people sang the *Magnificat* in gratitude for having known him. When Father Cousineau, barely able to control the tears in his voice, spoke to them of Brother André's life, of his untiring work and his supernatural devotion to God and Mary and Joseph, they wept with him.

Throughout the days and nights that followed the crowds never ceased to file past the tiny body lying between tall candles and guarded by his faithful friends, the firemen of Montreal. The waiting lines stretched down the mountainside, people standing with endless patience in the sleet and rain, or kneeling on the slippery steps. Father Cousineau estimated that 75,000 people passed the coffin every twenty-four hours.

Among those who came to the Crypt on the fourth day was Mme. Ducharme, who brought her little son, Arthur Ducharme. The child had smashed his arm in an accident. All efforts to repair it through surgery had failed; it was paralyzed and seemed on the point of mortification from lack of circulation. It happened that Arthur Saint-Pierre had come that day to venerate Brother André. Hear his testimony before the Tribunal:

"I was in the sacristy of the Oratory when Madame Ducharme and her son entered it as they left Brother André's remains. Madame Ducharme was extraordinarily moved, though she retained her dignity. Weeping she told me that her son had been suddenly cured as he touched Brother André. This was confirmed by an attendant from the Hospital of Saint Jean who was there to give first aid, and by many other people who were present.

"I heard from these people that the child was suddenly able to move his arm freely, and that he proved he could lift weights with it by carrying chairs around. . . . All that remained of his accident was a certain stiffness of the hand which Dr. Bazin afterward described as "wrist-drop." However, that hand retained its vigor. . . . In fact the child used his hand to play hockey, an extremely violent sport, without any inconvenience.

"I was so impressed by the character of this cure that I decided to make an investigation of the circumstance. I saw Dr. F. H. Gatien [who had taken care of him]. He confirmed the testimony of the child's mother on the gravity of the accident and the fact that he had urged the necessity for an amputation. . . ."

However, Dr. Gatien refused to attest the cure on the legalistic ground that it was not complete because Brother André had not cured the "wrist-drop."

There were other sudden cures while Brother André lay between the tall candles in front of the wall full of braces and crutches of those he had healed. More important from a spiritual standpoint, there were so many conversions that they remain uncounted save by God.

On the third day Brother André was taken in procession to the Cathedral of Montreal. In wind-driven, blinding rain the cortege moved slowly along Côte-des-Neiges and down the steep slope to the city. His stalwart firemen were his pallbearers, making two lines beside the hearse, while thousands of people— "many of them women in their little shoes"—followed it on foot through the icy downpour; and thousands more knelt in the streets. Even the great cathedral could not contain the crowd. The Vicar General, Monseigneur Georges Chartier, chanted the Requiem Mass for Brother André and Archbishop Gauthier pronounced the Absolution. As the last prayer was said the crowd rushed forward to venerate the casket and the last object he had touched.

On the way back the cortege turned through the wrought-iron gates of the College of Notre Dame. The firemen carried the little coffin into the building and set it down in the stiffly furnished parlor whose floor Brother André had so often washed. When it was opened the few remaining associates of his days as a porter looked down at the serene face they remembered chiefly for its laughter. Father Clément, whom he had cured of blindness, was there, and Brother Coderre, who sometimes took his place at the door when he wanted to pray in the chapel. Very frail with age was Brother Abundius who had built the primitive shrine. All the other religious of the college paid him tribute, and then came the boys, successors to those he had played with and barbered and cured so long ago, looking with grave young eyes at his still face, touching his clothing or his hair for a spark of grace to take with them through life.

Then they all accompanied him up the mountain for the last time, where once again he was placed in the chapel surrounded by "a forest of *ex-votos.*"

During the next three days the crowd of pilgrims grew ever denser. They came by train and bus and plane from the whole continent. Of the final day Brother Placide wrote: "At the foot of the hill the automobiles rumbled all night like the thunder of a steel mill. The trolley cars kept running as close together as they could, bringing thousands and thousands of people to the gates, and already the grounds of the Oratory were filled to overflowing. The regular trolleys were insufficient and the tramway company recalled ancient wrecks from years of retirement and pressed them into service.

"So it was throughout the night, that formidable swarm of humanity constantly multiplying. It is estimated that 300,000 people arrived between Monday noon and Tuesday morning. All this feverish anxiety, this surge of people, can be understood by the words, often said, always the same, 'We must see Brother André!'

"But what was so mysterious as to be almost inconceivable, which, indeed, touched on the miraculous, was that over this turmoil reigned an atmosphere of grace, of peace, of holy exaltation. Truly the Spirit of God moved over that ocean of people; divine grace was here in palpable form; and one would have been soulless indeed not to feel intensely in the innermost fibers of his being the tangible presence of the supernatural. We all felt ourselves transformed, full of mutual love, a divine wind blew over us, 'and God has visited His people.' "

An altogether remarkable happening was that, although Brother André's body had not been embalmed, it suffered no change during the week it lay in state. Father Cousineau testified: "His face was calm and serene, its ascetic features seemingly accentuated. . . . About the fourth or fifth day I happened to say to a doctor, whose name I cannot recall, that

Brother André's body was still supple. Over the protests of the doctor, he and I examined Brother André and the doctor was amazed that the hands and the feet of the cadaver were still flexible. The body remained in this perfect condition until it was interred on January twelfth."

On Monday evening an attempt was made to open a passage through the crowd so that Cardinal Villeneuve, Archbishop of Quebec, could make a vigil by the casket. It proved impossible. The Cardinal observed to Father Cousineau, "I have often read in the lives of the saints that so great a concourse of people came to view their remains that the high prelates could not get near them. I always thought it was a pious exaggeration, but yesterday evening it was proved to me it could be authentic."

So came the morning of the seventh day, and the end of the long vigil. The people still filed past the foot of the coffin lightly touching Brother André's tiny feet. Outside, the terraces and roadways and the bleak ungraded hillside above the Crypt were engulfed by a sea of people, thousands of whom still stood in line hopeful of seeing Brother André. Just before the Mass the coffin was carried out of doors so that these people should not be disappointed of their last farewell to the little brother. Then it was brought again into the Crypt and placed before the altar. Protectingly above it was the white marble statue of Saint Joseph with its golden aureole gleaming in the light of many candles.

The Crypt was packed to its last inch of space with people, some of whom had been waiting there since Monday afternoon. Squeezed in among them were the Canadian dignitaries who had come to honor Brother André—The Canadian Secretary of State, Prime Minister Maurice Duplessis of Quebec, Mayor Adhémar Raynault of Montreal, and official representatives of half the provinces and cities of Canada beside the high dignitaries of the Church.

There were few emblems of mourning in the Crypt that day; nor were the people somber; joyous rather, for they believed, all of them were certain, that Brother André had already achieved "the eternal day of infinite bliss."

The solemn Mass was sung by Monseigneur Eugène Limoges, Bishop of Mont-Laurier. Before giving the Absolution, Cardinal Villeneuve expressed his own deep feelings and those of that congregation. "Whatever the reputation for virtue her children may have," he said, "the Church ordains that at all funeral services we must pray for their forgiveness for the human frailties they may have committed during their lives; and the Church forbids us to anticipate the judgment which she reserves to herself concerning the heroism of their life and the certainty of their entrance into heaven. With due respect for this prudence of the Holy Church, we may nevertheless say that this morning we celebrate the feast of humility.

"On the tomb which will hold the venerated remains of the apostle of Saint Joseph, Brother André, you will read three words: *Pauper, Servus et Humilis: Pauper,* poor, the religious whom you came here to see so many times: *Servus,* servant, the lay brother in the lowest rank of his community: *Humilis,* humble, so small in his own eyes that he never suspected the greatness of his work, and he always disregarded his ability to draw great crowds.

"And this recalls to our thoughts another poor and obscure man, Saint Joseph, husband of Mary, whom God chose to guard the virginity of his Mother and protect the divinity of his Son. See then the man whom Saint Joseph has chosen not only to build this basilica in his honor, but to spread the devotion which has filled our people these past thirty years.

"From Brother André to Saint Joseph let us mount yet higher, let us go to Christ himself, who descending from heaven was born in a manger to save the world. Here is true Christianity. For it is to humility that you have come to render homage, and it is the doctrine of humility which we celebrate today.

"You the humble ones of earth, you who suffer and who work . . . as you return to your daily labors and to your burdens and sorrows, think of the divine seal which the Lord places on a humble life. Remember that no prince of the Church, or of the world, could hope to have a funeral which gave rise to such deep feeling in our hearts as they hold today. Continue, then, to listen to the voice of the humble servant of God who says to you, 'Go to Joseph!' "

After this the Cardinal pronounced the Absolution. It is customary at the end of the service to sing the hymn *In Paradisum,* which beseeches the angels to carry the soul to heaven. In the tremendous stress of emotion this was *forgotten.* Afterward this accidental omission seemed significant since not a person there but was convinced that this sweet duty had already been performed.

After the Mass Brother André was removed to the sacristy back of the chapel. His fireman friend Léopold Lussier was there to help. "I had to pass a big piece of cloth beneath his body," he said, "which could be used for relics in case the Church some day confirmed his saintliness." The coffin was placed on boards over the tomb of waterproof cement which had been prepared in the southeast wall of the Crypt. Bishop Gauthier opened the coffin once more and looked into Brother André's face. Then he placed at his feet a lead tube containing a parchment scroll with the words, "Here repose the remains of Alfred Bessette in religion Brother André, of the Congregation of Holy Cross. . . ."

The lid of the copper-lined casket was screwed shut and it was covered with black cloth. This was bound with copper wire, around and across, upon which Chancellor Albert Valois fixed the great seal of Archbishop Gauthier. The casket was then lowered into the cement tomb, which was later covered with black, polished granite, the gift of Prime Minister Duplessis.

Archbishop Gauthier spoke the last solemn prayers as the cement tomb was sealed to await the final verdict of the Church on the saintliness of Brother André.

It seemed that the attention of the whole troubled world had been centered on Mount Royal during that January week. Throughout North America and even as far away as France and Italy and England people felt a sense of personal loss which was expressed in all their news media. Father Cousineau told the Tribunal that "More than three hundred and seventy newspapers published articles on the occasion of Brother André's death, all of them praising the virtues and especially the charity of the Servant of God. . . . More than three hundred of these journals were either Protestant or non-sectarian."

In this vast tide of laudation every possible word of praise was said. Things that Brother André would have been astounded to hear; things he would have angrily denied; things that he might shyly have admitted. Yet it remained for *Le Droit* of Ottawa to say the words he might have liked the best:

Brother André, little Brother, we shall miss you.

CHAPTER SEVENTEEN

The Cause of Brother André

SACRED CONGREGATION OF RITES
Cardinal Clemente Micara, Protector
MONTREAL
For the Beatification and Canonization
of the Servant of God
BROTHER ANDRÉ
(in the world Alfred Bessette) of
The Congregation of Holy Cross
Proposal
For the Introduction of The Cause

ARCHBISHOP CHARBONNEAU of Montreal felt that Brother André's holy life deserved the recognition of the Church and that his beatification and canonization would be for the greater glory of God and would spread devotion to Saint Joseph. Father Cousineau was certain of it. It was for these reasons that after the death of Brother André the Archbishop gave orders that an informal investigation concerning the possibility of his canonization be begun. He also directed that all the brother's meager belongings including his clothes, bed coverings, books, cooking utensils and, in fact, everything he had touched, be preserved so that if the Pope eventually declared him a saint, they might be used as relics for the veneration of the faithful.

[185]

On the night of January 6, 1937, only a short time after he died, it was decided to remove Brother André's heart and preserve it as an object of inspiration and possible veneration. Dr. Lamy testified:

I declare that on January 6, 1937, between eight and nine o'clock in the morning at the Hospital of Notre-Dame-de-l'Espérance at Saint Laurent, assisted by Doctor Riopel, an anatomical pathologist of the Hotel-Dieu of Montreal, I excised the heart of Brother André. The heart was placed in a vial in a special solution. The vial was sealed in the presence of many witnesses . . . [including] Father Alfred Charron, C.S.C., Superior Provincial, and Father Albert Cousineau, C.S.C., Rector of Saint Joseph's Oratory.

I later saw the vial containing the heart of Brother André placed behind a little grille in the sacristy of Saint Joseph's Oratory. I know that later Brother André's heart was moved to the office where Brother André used to receive his visitors.

I have nothing further to state, correct or explain in the testimony I have given before this Tribunal.

JOSEPH LIONEL LAMY

Early in 1937, Father Henri Paul Bergeron, C.S.C., began the exhaustive research for his biography of Brother André. At the same time other confreres began the arduous task of ringing doorbells and interviewing thousands of possible witnesses, and selecting those who could contribute the most information when and if an official tribunal should be set up. A careful search was made for letters or other writings of Brother André which produced only the two letters to his family previously mentioned. Since the Servant of God was a religious, all the religious houses in the diocese were requested to bring forward any information they might have regarding him.

At the same time the medical bureau which had been established at the Oratory under the direction of Dr. Lamy was meticulously investigating the marvelous cures that were taking place there, which the grateful beneficiaries attributed to the intercession of Brother André. Canon law requires proof of at least two miracles if eyewitnesses testify, and three or more if there is only hearsay and documentary evidence. With literally hundreds of marvelous cures to choose from only those which could be proved to the hilt were considered.

As finally collated for submission to the Holy See, the proofs of only one of these "miracles" (the cure of a woman suffering from cancer) consisted of a book of approximately 150 pages of closely spaced typing—the others were equally well documented. The narrative was in Latin, but the testimony and documents were in the original languages of the witnesses (in this case French and English).

The first section of this book described the nature of the cure. Then came the sworn testimony of the person cured. The seriousness of the illness was established by the testimony of three doctors, one of whom was an eminent specialist. They were followed by other witnesses from the hospital, and eyewitnesses of the cure, eighteen in all. This was buttressed by the records of the case from the files of the hospital, which included X-rays, analysis of all matter and pus, and the result of a biopsy made shortly before the cure.

Within two days after the cure had taken place the woman had returned to the hospital and submitted to another exhaustive series of tests which confirmed the cure. Later tests showed that it was permanent. Since the Holy See is most particular about the proof of cures, none could be considered in which the medical records were not taken immediately before and immediately afterward. Finally came the proof that the cure was attributed to the intercession of Brother André.

Equally methodical and minute procedures were followed to establish all the facts of Brother André's life even during the preliminary investigation. Quite literally thousands of articles about Brother André in newspapers and journals were examined and all the pertinent documents and records were photostated and attested. Everything was done in accordance with canon law and custom.

Another very important matter, indeed a crucial one, was the question of *non cultus*. In order to preserve to the Pope the final authority in these matters it is absolutely required that no official veneration or anything suggesting it be paid to the Servant of God. The spontaneous veneration of the people is allowed, and is even essential to proof of his fame and sanctity, but this must not be abetted by the clergy. In Brother André's case this spontaneous cult was so great as to prove embarrassing to the diocesan authorities. In order to eliminate any suggestion of official encouragement it was decided to remove the heart of Brother André from its rather conspicuous place in the sacristy.

Oratory of Saint Joseph of Mount Royal
Montreal, August 17, 1939

To H. E. MONSEIGNEUR E. A. DESCHAMPS,
Auxiliary Bishop at Montreal
MOST REVEREND EXCELLENCY

Permit me to propose to you a project which concerns the memory of our dear Brother André, C.S.C. Until the present time, with the permission of H. E. Monseigneur Gauthier, his heart has been conserved in the sacristy in a glass vase which all the faithful can see and touch.

But, as more and more visitors have learned of its location they have totally invaded the sacristy to such an extent that the priests cannot find a place to robe themselves in their sacerdotal vestments. What is more, the pilgrims, bishops and priests suppose its disposition there to be an invitation to render a public cult to Brother André, and they think that this might prejudice his beatification.

After consulting with the Superior General, Father Cousineau, I propose the following solution:

1. To remove Brother André's heart to the place where he received the pilgrims for so many years, that is to the office near the souvenir shop.

[188]

2. Protect this precious souvenir with great care against fire and theft.

3. Preserve the exact appearance of the office that it had when Brother André occupied it. . . .

If Brother André occupied this place in other times it was because it was accessible to everyone. It appears to me that the same motive gives value to placing his heart in the midst of his dear clients.

> I remain,
> Your respectful son in J. M. and J.
> EMILE DEGUIRE, C.S.C.

Even this was not deemed sufficient, as the following document dated 5 January, 1944, included in the Summation of the Cause indicates.

After describing the original location of Brother André's tomb in the Crypt, it continues:

> In order to avoid anything which could be considered as an invitation to a public cult, it was judged prudent to modify this state of affairs. Wartime conditions making it impossible to construct a sepulcher in the rock of the mountain, the religious of the Oratory have built a temporary sepulcher near the cliff, facing the place where the tomb originally was located. This sepulcher is closed by solid doors made of wood two and one half inches thick. Little decorative bays in the doors facilitate ventilation. Four small lamps fastened to the dark brick walls discretely light the place.
>
> It was on the fifth day of January, 1944, at half past seven in the evening that I, the undersigned Archbishop of Montreal, in the presence of the Very Reverend Father Albert Cousineau, Superior General of the Congregation of Holy Cross . . . and many religious and the Chancellor of our diocese, after having blessed the sepulcher, transported a distance of twelve feet three inches without opening it, the sealed cement tomb containing . . . the remains of Alfred Bessette, in religion Brother André, of the Congregation of Holy Cross.
>
> JOSEPH CHARBONNEAU, Archbishop of Montreal.

After the war Brother André's tomb was enclosed in a small votive chapel to Saint Joseph, where it now rests.

On November 13, 1940, the Archbishop opened an official inquiry; and the Tribunal held its first hearing late in 1940. Over a period of nine years it questioned and cross-examined forty-nine witnesses at 293 sessions and studied a vast number of documents. A tremendous weight of evidence supported the propositions of the Vice Postulator that:

Art. 1 —*It is the truth that* Brother André was born on the ninth of August 1845, that he was baptised the next day.

Art. 2 —*It is the truth that* Brother André had Christian parents. . . . [Where articles that are proved are omitted for reasons of space, omission is indicated by dots. . . .]

Art. 7 —*It is the truth that* he was a pious child, a mortified young man united to God in prayer.

Art. 8 —*It is the truth that* from his childhood he had a special devotion to Saint Joseph.

Art.　—*It is the truth that* when 25 years old he entered the Congregation of Holy Cross where he took the name of Brother André. . . .

Art. 15 —*It is the truth that* his faith was manifested by his devotion to the Holy Eucharist, to the Mass, to Communion.

Art. 16 —*It is the truth that* his faith was manifested by his devotion to the Blessed Virgin.

Art. 17 —To the Passion of Our Lord.

Art. 18 —To Saint Joseph. . . .

Art. 22 —*It is the truth that* in 1904 a small chapel to Saint Joseph was built on the slope of the mountain.

Art. 23 —*It is the truth that* pilgrims begin to come in crowds and their numbers do not cease to increase. . . .

Art. 25 —*It is the truth that* due to his perseverance and faith a magnificent Oratory is being erected. . . .

Art. 33 —*It is the truth that* whether in joy or sorrow he referred all things to God. . . .

Art. 34 —*It is the truth that* he exhorted others to be confident.

Art. 35 —*It is the truth that* he would face death with joy.

Art. 36 —*It is the truth that* he loved God with all his heart.
. . .

Art. 47 —*It is the truth that* during his prayers prodigious
phenomena sometimes occurred. . . .

Art. 58 —*It is the truth that* he abhorred idleness. . . .

Art. 74 —*It is the truth that* he was sometimes molested by the
demon. . . .

Art. 81 —*It is the truth that* his chastity was admirable. . . .

Art 91 —*It is the truth that* he could read in the spirits of men.

Art. 92 —*It is the truth that* he sometimes predicted future
events.

Art. 93 —*It is the truth that* he stated things which he could
not possibly have known without divine intervention.

Art. 94 —*It is the truth that* he would cure the sick.

Art. 95 —*It is the truth that* during his lifetime men of honesty
and piety, priests, bishops, even non-Catholics considered
him a saint. . . .

Art. 103 —*It is the truth that* he died calmly and simply as he
had lived. . . .

Art. 103 —*It is the truth that* news of his death was spread as
would be that of the death of a saint. . . .

Art. 110 —*It is the truth that* even after his death he still obtains favors for those who invoke him.

Such was the opinion of the Tribunal in the Archdiocese of
Montreal. It was in no way binding on the Holy See. How-
ever, they were compelling in the decision of Archbishop
Joseph Charbonneau of Montreal (who had succeeded the late
Bishop Gauthier) to submit the Cause of Brother André to the
Sacred Congregation of Rites in Rome. The Advocate of the
Cause in Rome later observed, "The whole body of proof on
which this Cause is based is indeed even more full and more
detailed than is required."

In July, 1950, all the documents were packed in a small
square trunk, which was carefully locked and sealed. Among
its contents were 242 letters from six cardinals and numerous

archbishops, bishops, superiors, mothers superior, and distinguished laymen, requesting the Holy Father to consider the Cause of Brother André. The first letter follows:

FROM THE MOST EMINENT LORD CARDINAL FRANCIS SPELLMAN, ARCHBISHOP OF NEW YORK

31 May, 1946.

MOST HOLY FATHER:

It is with deep respect that I beg permission to commend to Your Holiness the advisability of the canonization of Brother André Bessette, a lay brother of the Congregation of Holy Cross. The belief in the holiness of his life is widespread among our people. During the long period that Brother André was attached to the Shrine of Saint Joseph in Montreal thousands of the faithful of this diocese visited it each year, attracted by the fame of sanctity of this pious lay brother. I feel certain that all these people wish me to intercede with Your Holiness in favor of this good brother being publicly recognized as a man of extraordinary virtue and an instrument chosen by God to stimulate the devotion to Saint Joseph in our part of the world.

As I most humbly kiss the feet of Your Holiness and express to you my most sincere filial devotion, I sign myself,

The most humble servant of Your Holiness,

FRANCIS, CARDINAL SPELLMAN,
Archbishop of New York

The trunk containing the documents was flown to Rome by two eminent *coursiers* appointed by Archbishop Charbonneau, Father Alfred Laplante and Father Cousineau. At the Vatican, guarded by halberd-bearing members of the Swiss Guard in brilliant broad-striped uniforms and plumed helmets, they ceremoniously delivered it to Monseigneur René Fontenelle, who had been appointed Postulator of the Cause, and Father Edward L. Heston, C.S.C.

For eight years more the officials appointed by the Sacred Congregation of Rites studied the documents. First they were copied in handwriting by the Vatican copyists, and the originals returned to the archives of the Archdiocese of Montreal. Then the Protector of the Cause, Cardinal Micara; the Postulator, Monseigneur Fontenelle; and the Promoter General of the Faith, Salvator Natucci, together with the Advocate, Procurator, Sub-Promoter, and other officials, subjected them to intensive scrutiny.

In 1957, Monseigneur Fontenelle died and Father Heston was appointed Postulator in his place, by the Very Reverend Christopher J. O'Toole, Superior General of Holy Cross, with the approval of the Sacred Congregation. The new Postulator, who had been Monseigneur Fontenelle's right-hand man, was thoroughly conversant with all the disciplines of the Vatican. A man of indomitable energy, he also held the offices of Procurator General, Counselor of the Sacred Congregation for Religious, and Commissary of the Holy Office and of the Sacred Congregation of the Sacraments. In fact, he was not only expert Advocate but was qualified by a great enthusiasm for Brother André. The latter's confreres in Canada, who were praying daily for the success of the Cause, rightly felt that it could not be in better hands.

Finally, in 1958, it was ready to be presented to the cardinals of the Sacred Congregation of Rites for the all-important vote on whether it had sufficient merit to be referred to the Pope for introduction to the Court of Rome. Knowing that a brilliant oration may sway the minds of men beyond the just deserts of the matter, canon law does not permit the arguments to be presented orally. However, even in cold type the Advocate's opening statement for Brother André was very moving:

The Sacred Congregation of Rites.
The most Eminent and Reverend LORD CARDINAL CLEMENTE MICARA, Protector:
1. Although minds are attracted in admiration of remarkable goodness joined to knowledge and doctrine, those qualities which shine forth from simplicity and openness of soul are even more compellingly attractive to us. For this sort of sim-

THE CAUSE OF BROTHER ANDRÉ

plicity is to be considered as the highest wisdom, especially as it is appointed not to teach, but rather to love in the hidden places of the cloister. Such men are not appointed by God to govern others, but rather are designated to provide them with examples of obedience. It is they who become as little children, and in them are manifest heavenly graces scarcely to be excelled by literary fame or earthly knowledge. . . .

2. The humble lay brother whose Cause is now proposed, was formed and perfected by the distinguished Congregation of Holy Cross. In our own time he was recognized for many years by the people of Canada . . . as a pauper among the poor, inexhaustible in his love for them; and his reputation for holiness was acknowledged among them. Those who benefited by his aid in their necessities, even in his own lifetime, erected a shrine to Saint Joseph in Montreal which is famous throughout America, as a lasting memorial of the life which Brother André gave to God's glory and the salvation of souls.

Since the death of the Servant of God, the belief of men in his holiness has been increased and strengthened by the divine evidence of prodigies granted at his intercession, prodigies which indicate that God's humble servant, whose place here was so low, we now see raised on high.

3. It seems therefore fitting that this fame of holiness, which each year grows and spreads, should now be given the supreme sanction; for nothing will be of greater use to our own proud era than that this example of love, humility and poverty in the person of Brother André be held up as an example to all so that they may learn to know true salvation, light and peace.

The statement in favor of Brother André continued for ninety-one pages of closely reasoned argument buttressed by quotations from the testimony and documents. Its final section follows:

62. Conclusion. Since all that I have discussed in the preceding chapters concerning the life and good works of Brother André not only demonstrates his true fame of sanctity, but also, in my humble opinion, it is all that is required at this stage of

the investigation to prove his heroic virtue I am led to believe
that the Commission for the introduction of the Cause may be
duly approved.

For it appears that this matter would redound to the greater
glory of God's name, and to an increase in Faith and Charity
of which there is such an immense need today. . . .

HUGO SERAFINI
Advocate.
MICHAEL D'ALFONSO
Procurator.

The next section of the Proceedings is entitled: "Animadversions, by the Promoter General of the Faith."

It consists of twenty-nine pages of objections raised by the
Devil's Advocate as was his duty as Promoter or Protector of
the Faith. These objections range all the way from slight irregu-
larities in the conduct of the Canadian tribunals through the
vast preponderance of favorable witnesses; the old objections
to Brother André by the doctors of Montreal; the occasional ir-
ritability of the Servant of God; his absences from the community; every possible little blemish in his life, to the final
objection that he did not request Extreme Unction on his
deathbed—he was, of course, unconscious.

One begins to feel that this Devil's Advocate is indeed a
captious and critical fellow. Then comes the final paragraph
which proves that his heart is, after all, in the right place and
that he was only doing his duty:

> I have now said enough; and I will conclude with the hope
> that the skillful Patron of the Servant of God will be able to
> vindicate him from these objections; nothing could be more
> desirable to me, nothing could please me more, because of the
> regard in which I hold this pious and lovable old man, this
> disciple of Saint Joseph.
>
> All things, however, are set forth according to the rule.
> SALVATOR NATUCCI, Advocate of the Sacred Congregations
> Promoter General of the Faith.

[195]

In the rebuttal, entitled "Response to the Animadversions," which occupies one hundred twenty-seven pages, the Advocate neatly demolished these objections, as indeed the kind Devil's Advocate hoped that he would. Having done so he wrote:

> It appears most opportune that the Cause of beatification of the humble André be discussed at this time, it now being fifty years since the foundation of the original simple Shrine of Saint Joseph. Today, mainly because of his work and zeal, the Shrine has become a great temple standing on the summit of Mount Royal in the city of Montreal, from which light goes out over all America, and indeed one could say to the whole terrestrial globe. This clear, spiritual light continually beckons and draws from everywhere great throngs of pilgrims, as well as a considerable number of infidels, who are seeking a haven of salvation. All this is certainly definite and enduring testimony to the great apostolate of the Servant of God, who sought to praise the Most High and to help men attain spiritual and temporal well being. . . .

Now the Cause was placed before the cardinals of the Sacred Congregation of Rites. After careful study of all the documents the Congregation brought the matter to a vote on April 15, 1958.

The great chamber of the Vatican where the Congregation met was both beautified and inspired by works of religious art by the great masters of the Renaissance. Gathered there were not only the cardinals of the Congregation but all the officials and consultants appointed by them to take part in the deliberations. Three votes were taken. The first two were purely advisory and consultants as well as cardinals took part. On the final ballot the cardinals alone voted on the question of whether the Cause of Brother André was worthy to be submitted to the Pope with the view of introducing it in the Court of Rome.

The action of the Sacred Congregation of Rites was a giant step forward in the Cause of Brother André; but it was far from meaning that he would be automatically beatified. What it did mean was that the Cause had successfully weathered the stringent conditions laid down by the Sacred Congregation, and that the latter had solemnly judged whether or not it was worthy of consideration by the Pope himself.

Following the normal course of such things the Holy Father would soon sign the placet with his own hand. This will authorize what is called the Apostolic Process.

The matter is now taken out of the hands of the Archdiocese of Montreal and conducted directly by the Holy See. If the placet is issued, a new Tribunal responsible to Rome will be established in Montreal and Inquiry Commissions at other places, with judges, vice-postulator, sub-promoter of the Faith, and others, all *appointed by Rome.* Those witnesses who are still living will be recalled to testify.

This court will, in effect, review the proceedings of the Informative or Ordinary Process. By careful inquiry it will endeavor to confirm the heroism with which Brother André practiced the theological virtues and the four cardinal virtues. The question of *non cultus,* that there has been no *official* veneration of Brother André, will be the subject of extremely meticulous scrutiny. Then the proof of the miracles will be examined with great care.

In the course of the Apostolic Process Brother André's tomb will be opened and his remains will be "recognized" officially. When all this is completed the records will be sent to Rome, where the whole Process will again be examined by the officials and the Sacred Congregation of Rites. If it is approved, a general Congregation will be held in the presence of the Sovereign Pontiff. After the miracles have been acknowledged the doubt is formulated in the question, "Is it now possible to proceed to the beatification of the Servant of God?" If the vote of the consultants and cardinals is favorable, the Pope, if he also feels certain, will issue a decree to that effect.

Later, possibly many years later, the Process of Canonization may be begun. A document establishing formal beatification of the Servant of God is required to begin it. Then to proceed to the canonization of Brother André, there must be absolute proof of two miracles wrought through his intercession *after his beatification.*

When these conditions are fulfilled and approved by the Court of Rome, the Pope himself will consider the matter, studying the conclusions of men and seeking guidance from God in prayer. If the Holy Father is finally moved to proclaim the canonization of the Servant of God, a date for the event will be announced.

On that glorious day, if it ever comes, the Pope will be carried into the great Basilica of Saint Peter's in the *sedia gestatoria,* the huge white and gold sedan chair of ceremony, on the shoulders of his guards. In the presence of a great congregation gathered in the splendor of the greatest church in Christendom he will conduct one of the most moving and beautiful rites of the Church. At the conclusion of the ceremonies, ordered by ancient tradition and divine sanction, the Sovereign Pontiff will say, "In honor of the Holy and Undivided Trinity, for the exaltation of the Church and the growth of the Christian religion, with the authority of our Lord Jesus Christ, of the blessed apostles, Peter and Paul, and Our own; after mature deliberation and having frequently implored Divine Aid . . ." He will then decree and define that Brother André is a saint and he will order that he "be inscribed in the list of the saints, laying down that his memory be recalled with pious devotion every year . . . in the name of the Father and of the Son and of the Holy Spirit."

Saint Joseph's of Mount Royal

THERE were those of lesser faith who feared that when Brother André died the Work of the Oratory would slow down and finally stop. On the contrary! It surged forward in a splendid tide of piety and devotion. Almost on the morrow of his death, M. Claude came with a group of the little brother's friends to ask permission of Father Cousineau to come on the first Wednesday of every month for an hour of services in his memory. At their first meeting, not only were his faithful friends there, but a thousand people attended the function in the Crypt; and it has been crowded on those nights ever since. Nor did people forget his Holy Hour every Friday night.

Brother André was quite right when he said that if a statue of Saint Joseph were put in the Basilica he would soon find a roof for himself. Ten months after his death there was a roof over the nave, and the huge concrete dome was in place, seeming to float like a balloon above the massive structure of the Basilica.

In a daring flight of architectural imagination Dom Bellot had changed the original design, using modern construction techniques to save expense and at the same time create a feeling of lightness and grace. His dome is a hollow concrete monolith 125 feet in diameter which rises almost two hundred feet

[201]

above the central mass of the building. But the shell of this towering structure is so brilliantly engineered that its walls only need to be a few inches thick.

Father Bergeron described the joyful ceremony that took place when it was completed:

"On a cold autumn afternoon we went in procession to the apse of the Basilica, which was now covered. Before the statuette of Saint Joseph in the presence of about two hundred kneeling workmen we recited the Rosary, chanted the Litany of the Holy Patriarch and prayed for the glorification of Brother André. In a single year what a work had been accomplished; what success beyond all hope!"

However, though the dome was now in place, there were still grave anxieties. The engineers feared that the unprotected concrete would be seriously damaged by the rigorous Canadian winter. They shielded it temporarily as best they could and Saint Joseph did the rest; the dome came through unscathed. But it was vital to protect it for the future. The design called for it to be covered by copper sheathing. With World War II impending, copper prices were sky high and its use restricted by the Government. Again the seemingly impossible was accomplished. The copper was contributed in part by Americans; and the dome was covered.

When it was first sheathed in burnished copper the dome was a magnificent spectacle blazing in the afternoon light like a brilliant red-gold counterpart of the sun. There was thought of trying to keep it polished like that but the project, perhaps fortunately, proved impracticable. It soon began to tarnish in the weather, turning at first a dreadfully garish pea green. Gradually this faded to a soft, misty, bluish green that blended beautifully with the blue of the sky and the dark foliage of primeval trees on the mountain.

In 1940 the outdoor Way of the Cross was begun on the mountain. This was one of Brother André's dearest projects. He had said, "How many conversions will there be on the Way of the Cross on the Mountain! I think there will be more than in the Basilica."

As has been seen from the documents relating to Brother André's temporary tomb, the material and labor shortages of World War II slowed up the Work of the Oratory. However, in spite of the enormous difficulties the great stones which form an octagonal band of granite pierced by many windows at the base of the dome were hoisted one by one into place. It was completed in 1941. From the angle of each octagon, ribbed moldings of granite spring up the dome to form a pointed arch supporting the cupola and the lighted cross at its apex.

When the war ended in 1945, construction went forward with renewed vigor. The foundations of the Votive Chapel to Saint Joseph were literally hewn out of the rock of the mountain, and it was built enclosing Brother André's tomb. At about the same time a new office building was erected. It included a fine library specializing in all the works written about Saint Joseph in every language; and well-equipped editorial offices for *The Annals*. Thus, bit by bit the work of realizing Brother André's great dream goes forward. It is not yet completed, and will not be for a generation. Perhaps the work will never end, for such a project does not stand still, but so long as the divine inspiration is there it continues to grow and change.

Though still unfinished, Saint Joseph's of Mount Royal is today one of the greatest religious shrines in the world. People of the North American Continent sometimes wonder how it compares in size to the famous cathedrals of Europe. With the exception of Saint Peter's, it is second to none. The cross on the top of the dome is 361 feet above the floor of the Basilica, and because of the height of the mountain it is over five hundred feet above Queen Mary Road. This compares with the height of Saint Paul's in London, 365 feet, but the dome of Saint Paul's is only about 330 feet in circumference while Saint Joseph's is almost 400 feet. Other famous domes such as that of Sacré-Coeur in Paris and the Basilica of the Little Flower in Lisieux are much smaller. Even the tall slender spires of the great Gothic cathedrals seldom rise higher toward the heavens. Only Michelangelo's magnificent dome of Saint Peter's, 450 feet high and nearly 500 feet around, could really dwarf it.

Nor does the capacity of Saint Joseph's suffer by comparison with most of the great churches of Europe. Indeed, because of the clever way Dom Bellot designed the nave it can actually accommodate more of the faithful than most of them.

However, mere size obviously means nothing without beauty; and beauty must fail unless it also inspires faith. This Saint Joseph's does in a supreme manner. People who have been there and love it feel a lift of the heart, as they approach Montreal and see across fifty miles of flat green prairie the blue bubble of the dome rising above the darker blue of the Royal Mountain. Strangers may miss this first glimpse; but no one can fail to be inspired who stands before the tall gates on Queen Mary Road looking up the sweep of green lawns and terraces toward the great structure with its tiers of steps rising to balustraded esplanades and the great buildings on their different levels like a frozen cataract of granite leading the eye upward to the classically columned portico of the nave with its flanking towers, and onward up the great blue-green dome itself to the pointed cupola and soaring golden cross.

If the stranger then passes through the gates he first comes to Laliberté's heroic bronze statue of Saint Joseph on its high stone pediment, against which rise the tall pointed wings of four angels. From there the flower-bordered path leads to the long flight of steps that rise to the Crypt. Almost always there are kneeling pilgrims praying on each step, even on days of rain or snow. On either side is an automobile road for the infirm or those whose piety is not quite so great.

At the top of the steps is a broad terrace, with parking places and the pavilion restaurant to the south. Opening on it is the main entrance to the Crypt-Church, whose somberly impressive interior is almost exactly as it was in Brother André's time. From it the pilgrim goes under a fresco of the death of Saint Joseph through the archway where the brother's tomb first stood, into the Votive Chapel. This is a place of mystic dimness, lit by the dark red glow of vigil lamps. Saint Joseph, crowned and holding the crowned Infant, is at one end; the whole is dominated by a tall statue of the Patriarch at the top of a glowing parterre of lights said to contain three thousand votive lamps which are kept burning by the faithful who light them as a symbol of their wish to honor Saint Joseph.

On the walls of the Votive Chapel is a perfect forest of crutches and braces, canes and corsets contributed by those who joyously found they were no longer needed.

Behind the statue of Saint Joseph in an obscure niche is a polished, black granite sarcophagus on which is engraved simply: "Frère André C.S.C." But this is in fact the heart of the great shrine and all day and most of the night you will find pilgrims kneeling to pray for the intercession of the man whom *they* are sure is a saint.

From there the pilgrim begins his ascent of the mountain, not toiling upward as the faithful used to do, but carried swiftly up the interior of the Oratory on a series of remarkably fast escalators. On the second level is the museum of Brother André. Here are the two rooms in which he spent a great part of his life and the third in which he died. The first is an exact replica of the porter's cell at Notre Dame College with a wax figure of Brother André listening for his bell. The second is his "bourreau" in which the Servant of God, standing behind his counter, received and comforted so many unfortunates. The third is the white, wooden-walled room in which he died, transported board by board from the Hospital of the Sisters of Hope at Saint Laurent. In the white iron bedstead a waxen figure of Brother André lies with Father Cousineau's crucifix still on his breast.

On the opposite side of the room in its vase of steel and glass is Brother André's heart which stands as a symbol of his love of God and of his neighbor.

Another fast ascent brings the pilgrim to the permanent exhibitions. One of these depicts the life of Saint Joseph. A second is dedicated to the history of the cult of the Patriarch in Canada, while still another is given over to the great saints who were instrumental in propagating devotion to Saint Joseph throughout the world, such as Saints Theresa of Ávila and Francis of Sales.

The fourth and final escalator rises to the floor of the Basilica itself. The pillared portico at the top of a long bank of stone stairs commands the magnificent view of the great plain edged by the blue Laurentian Mountains and the distant glimmer of the Saint Lawrence and its tributary rivers to which Brother André loved to lift his eyes as he meditated or read his missal.

The interior of the church is no less majestic. From the great entrance doors to the chapel in the bay of the apse there is a clear vista of 325 feet, broken only by the main Altar of Sacrifice behind which rises an enormously tall carved wooden Calvary. It was originally intended to cast this moving representation of Christ in His Agony in bronze; but such is the beauty of the carving and the dramatic simplicity of the plain wooden figures standing amid the splendid marble walls that possibly the original model will be retained.

On either side of the long nave and the choir are massive piers from which spring the triple-columned arches that soar steeply up to support the hundred-foot-high ceiling and the interior cupola of the mighty dome which rises another ninety-five feet. The cupola is decorated with gold leaf and mosaics to form a canopy over the altar, while each of the twelve grooves in the pillars bears a proportionately tall statue of one of the Twelve Apostles.

The main altar is above all a simple Table of Sacrifice; it has no Tabernacle. A side chapel is reserved for the Blessed Sacrament. Custom was thus varied, in accordance with a recent pronouncement of the Sacred Congregation of Rites concerning large churches, so that the faithful who wish to adore the Eucharist are not disturbed by the services taking place in the sanctuary. This chapel, capable of accommodating several hundred people, is in one of the lower transepts. It is lighted by a tall stained-glass window. On an altar of pure white marble, around whose base are sculpted Christ's Disciples, stands the "Holy Tent," which is what the word "tabernacle" means. It is covered with gold and surrounded by adoring angels in bronze. A shining slender spire inlaid with colorful enamel surmounts the Tabernacle suggesting the Presence of the Divine Host. In dignity and splendor it was conceived by Jean Charles Charuest, a young Canadian artist.

The severe lines of the columns and arches, leading the eye upward to the immensity of the dome, combined with the richness of marble and gold and splendid color, make a visit to the Basilica an inspiring religious experience. However, as Brother André foretold, the Way of the Cross on the Mountain is the most beautiful and moving place of all.

The Stations of the Cross are placed along a path that winds up the mountain on the east side of the Basilica. The pilgrim first comes to the Grotto of Agony, a place hewn out of the living rock, where Jesus kneels before the Angel of the Lord to receive His Father's commands while three tired Disciples have fallen asleep outside.

At each Station the pilgrim finds a statue of Christ on His Sorrowful Way. In the heroic-scale figures, magnificently carved from pure limestone, the Canadian sculptor Louis Parent has combined the strong uncluttered lines of modern sculpture with a poignant sense of suffering and exaltation. Each of the fourteen Stations is placed in a small garden whose flowers are chosen to reflect by their color the emotions of the scene. For example, at the Third Station where Our Lord falls for the

[207]

first time beneath the weight of His Cross, the predominant color is red suggesting the flow of blood; and at the Station where Saint Veronica wipes the sweat and blood from the face of Christ, the colors are delicate pastels to remind us of her tender gesture.

As the pilgrim slowly climbs the steep winding path through the trees, pausing to pray and meditate at each Station, he is almost overcome by the sorrow that pierces his heart, and by love for our Lord who suffered so greatly for him. The last three Stations, the Death, the Descent from the Cross, and the Burial, would be unbearably tragic were it not for the sure knowledge of Glory to come.

Turning from the final Station, the pilgrim climbs the Triumphant Way, a steep flight of stairs leading straight up the mountain to the Monument of the Resurrection on the highest point of the garden. Here is the empty tomb with the great stone rolled away from its entrance and the Risen Christ "standing in all His eloquent majesty."

After the exalted emotion of this great pilgrimage comes serenity bestowed by the quiet of the exquisite garden and the magnificent view of the city and the plain. As the pilgrim descends he pauses by the Pool of the Redemption. Reflected in this mirrored sheet of water is a symbolic presentation of the Redemption of men by their Savior. Christ is represented by the figure of a lamb at the far end of the pool, from whose side flows a crystal stream of water—the water of grace. This is caught in a basin with seven founts symbolizing the Church, from which grace flows out through the seven sacraments into another basin which is emblematic of the faithful.

Too often in churches the worshipers hurry around the Stations of the Cross seeking to gain grace from a pious act perfunctorily performed with one eye on Heaven and the other on a wrist watch. It is impossible to scamp devotion on the Way of the Cross on the Mountain. So much beauty and spiritual in-spiration are spread before his eyes that even an infidel must pause and reflect on mysteries of faith beyond human knowl-edge.

In the Oratory grounds there are two other important ob-jects. The first of these is the carillon of fifty-six bells, the largest of which weighs 2,200 pounds. It is the third biggest carillon in all North America and eventually will become the largest when five more heavy bells are added. Originally it was cast by Paccard Brothers in France for the Eiffel Tower. When the Tower's engineers decided it was too heavy for the old steel girders, the Oratory bought it at a bargain. It is presently set up in a temporary building attached to the restaurant pavilion. When the plans are completed the bells will chime from a high campanile to be built especially for them.

On February 1, 1955, the bells were christened individually in a liturgical ceremony performed by twelve bishops and a number of monseigneurs, pastors, and religious superiors pre-sided over by Paul-Emile Cardinal Léger, Archbishop of Mont-real, who consecrated the largest bell himself. At that time the Cardinal said: "Because it is the exalted mission of bells to an-nounce God's presence they must be sanctified in the solemn ceremony known as 'the baptism of the bells.' In the future when you hear the ringing of the bells remember that it is a call from God, a call to prayer, a reminder of God's presence in the midst of the blind, restless activity of our times."

The final important place on the grounds is not the last, but the first. Brother André's original chapel has been moved a little to one side of its original location and higher up the mountain. It stands among a grove of trees, as indeed it always did. Its single white steeple and iron-sheathed wooden walls are a touching reminder of the small beginnings of this great enter-prise of faith on the mountain.

Throughout this work the great church on Mount Royal has been referred to as the "Basilica"; but it was not in fact entitled to that appellation until 1955. On Saint Joseph's Day, March 19 of that year, Cardinal Léger, in the name of Pope Pius XII, solemnly elevated Saint Joseph's Oratory of Mount Royal to its present rank at a Pontifical High Mass. Assisting at the Mass were six bishops, hundreds of prelates and religious and a vast congregation of the faithful. The Holy Father had written: "We have learned that Montreal, the metropolis of Canada, is magnificently graced by a vast and holy temple dedicated to Saint Joseph, spouse of the Mother of God. This august temple, known as Saint Joseph's Oratory of Mount Royal, measures some sixty-five paces in length by forty-one paces in width and rises majestically heavenward. . . ."

After speaking of the millions of pilgrims from far places who come to pray at the shrine, the Holy Father continued, "Desirous of augmenting yet more this trend of piety and devotion towards Saint Joseph, our beloved son, Paul-Emile Léger . . . has requested us to accord the name and rank of a minor Basilica to this temple. We grant this request willingly."

Thus the most beloved Pope of our time recognized the work of faith begun by Brother André.

The phrase minor Basilica might strike some people as odd in view of the magnitude and influence of Saint Joseph's. It is, however, a technical term delineating the privileges thus accorded. There are only seven Major Basilicas, all in Rome; and while the perquisites of a minor Basilica are not as great, neither are they insignificant. They include the right of precedence over other churches; and the rights to an *umbrellino,* a coat of arms and a special seal. Another privilege is that Saint Joseph's is entitled to have an officiating bishop wear the canonical *cappa,* a special vestment that can only be used in certain of the minor Basilicas.

However, all these things are but symbols of the importance which the Holy Father attached to the work of the Oratory.

The vital thing remains, as it was in Brother André's little shelter on the mountain, the spirit of devotion and the propagation of faith.

Saint Joseph's is owned and operated by the Congregation of Holy Cross. The religious of Holy Cross are of course responsible for its finances. Ordinary administrative matters are in charge of the Superior of the Oratory and his council. Matters of greater importance require the approval of the Superior Provincial of Holy Cross in Canada. However, if they want to build an addition costing more than $10,000 it must be approved by the Superior General of the Order in Rome. If the sum to be spent is over $50,000 permission must be obtained from the Holy See.

The Fathers of Holy Cross also own the little piece of land at Saint Grégoire on which stood the cabin where Brother André was born. Unfortunately the house burned down in 1925. In 1945 an impressive monument was erected to his memory by the local unit of the Saint John the Baptist Society which presented it to the congregation. It is a gigantic granite cross standing amid the open fields where Brother André played as a boy. On the pediment below the cross is a statue of Saint Joseph holding the Christ Child. Every year on Brother André's birthday great crowds gather there for the service in his memory.

The operation of the Oratory is indeed a vast undertaking. Far from falling off throughout the years the number of pilgrims and visitors has steadily increased until the average is now some three million a year. Just taking care of the material needs of this multitude is no small job. Much more important and exacting are their spiritual necessities. True, the character of the place itself ministers to these, but the religious of Holy Cross must be ever ready to provide comfort and hope for the sick and forlorn; advice for troubled souls; atonement for sinners; and be vigilant that no opportunity to regain a straying lamb or make a convert be lost. In other words they must do on a far grander scale all the things which Brother André did alone.

On each Wednesday of the month the sick from one of the four quarters of the metropolitan area are brought to the Oratory to pray, to be blessed and, perhaps, to be healed. They arrive by the hundreds in private automobiles loaned by their owners, in buses and in ambulances. Brother André's old friends, the firemen, turn out in their smart blue uniforms to help handle the crowds and carry the stretchers into the Crypt where the Benediction is given. During the service the consecrated Host is carried around the church for all to adore.

Afterward the unfortunates usually feel like saying a prayer at Brother André's tomb. Many are disappointed, but thousands are helped. For manifestations of divine favors have continued to be received through the years. From the time of Brother André's death in 1937, until September, 1958, people have reported 41,504 cures and 98,211 favors granted through the intercession of Saint Joseph and Brother André. Those who attribute their cures directly to the intercession of Brother André number 31,932, while the favors granted through him are reported to number 61,109.

Following the trend of modern Catholicism to adapt modern methods to the service of God, the priests and brothers of Holy Cross who staff the Oratory make use of all appropriate mechanical means to accomplish their work. The Oratory has its own automobiles to speed them about their business. Some of these can be converted into ambulances. It has its own post office to handle the enormous volume of mail—7,801,051 letters were received between 1925 and September, 1958. *"The Annals of Saint Joseph,* in French and English, has a circulation comparable to that of a large American national magazine, and its editorial offices are as well equipped. The library, to which scholars come from all over the world to do research on Saint Joseph, is beautifully and conveniently arranged and catalogued. The Mass is broadcast every Sunday from the Basilica as are other special services. Splendid documentary films about the history and activities of the Oratory have been produced in various languages and are circulated throughout the world. On the staff also is an expert photographer who is supplied with a dark room and the most modern equipment of that trade.

These are only a few of the numerous and complex operations of the Oratory. Since there is no time to be wasted on their Master's business, the staff usually functions at a dead run from five thirty in the morning until late in the evening, just as Brother André used to do when he was the porter at Notre Dame.

The Superior who is at present in charge of all these activities is the Reverend Father Roland Gauthier. A gentle and ascetic priest, he has a rather frail appearance, delicate features and the eyes of an intellectual mystic. So he is, but he is also an excellent executive because this, too, is necessary.

On the days of the great special pilgrimages the Oratory receives the faithful on a grand scale. Such a day was Sunday, June 15, 1958, when some 50,000 members of the Sacred Heart League made a formal pilgrimage to Saint Joseph's. Contingents came from all parts of Canada and the United States. The grounds of the shrine were decked out to receive them. All along the grassy central mall the pennants of the Sacred Heart flew from tall poles. At the top of the long flight of steps in front of the Crypt a platform was erected for the open-air Mass, on either side of which flew the white and gold banner of the Church and the blue and white flag bearing the Lilies of France which is the standard of the Province of Quebec. Marching behind their bands and standards and singing hymns in honor of the Eucharistic Heart of Jesus, the Sacred Heart Leagues mounted the slope in the bright June sunshine. As each arrived in front of the Crypt its standard bearer was sent to the roof. The parapet and bastions lined by hundreds of deep red banners looked like a medieval fortress during a royal visit.

In mid-afternoon Cardinal Léger arrived standing up in an

open automobile with his red robe whipping in the brisk wind as he blessed the people. After inspirational addresses by Canadian Minister of Justice Davie Fulton and Senator Cyrille Vaillancourt, the Cardinal celebrated Mass in the open air.

Meanwhile small confessionals had been set up along all the driveways and the lower parking space. They were manned by over two hundred priests who heard the confessions of thousands of people who wished to receive Communion. When the Host was consecrated, these priests carried golden chalices through the crowds giving Communion to all who wished to receive it. Over 20,000 of the faithful took Communion that day.

The Feast of the Sacred Heart was only one, and not the largest, of the special ceremonies that were held at Saint Joseph's during the year. Even on days of no religious significance the grounds of the Oratory were crowded with pilgrims. At night when the pilgrims all have left the great floodlit dome with its illuminated cross visible throughout the city and across fifty miles of prairie sends its silent message of devotion to all who raise their eyes. Thus from the pilgrims by day and its majestic beauty by night the influence of the Oratory spreads out in ripples of faith over all the North American Continent.

The vast range of its influence is not due to its size and splendor; not even to its lovely lines and superb setting on the mountain. For though beauty and pageantry exalt the human soul they alone cannot lead it to the sublime heights which it may attain. The Oratory on Mount Royal does this because the spirit of little Brother André seems to burn within it like a vigil lamp before the statue of Saint Joseph.

Nihil obstat
> RT. REV. MSGR. PETER B. O'CONNOR
> *Censor librorum*

Imprimatur
> MOST REVEREND THOMAS A. BOLAND, S.T.D.,
> *Archbishop of Newark*

The Size of the Oratory

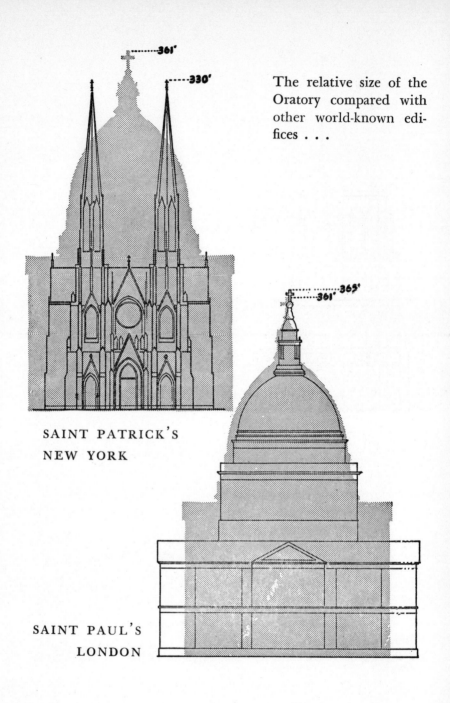

361'

330'

The relative size of the
Oratory compared with
other world-known edi-
fices . . .

SAINT PATRICK'S
NEW YORK

365'
361'

SAINT PAUL'S
LONDON

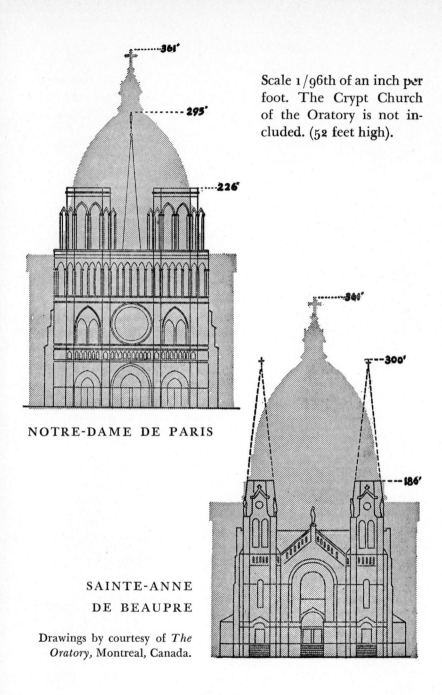

Scale 1/96th of an inch per foot. The Crypt Church of the Oratory is not included. (52 feet high).

NOTRE-DAME DE PARIS

SAINTE-ANNE
DE BEAUPRE

Drawings by courtesy of *The Oratory*, Montreal, Canada.

Index

INDEX